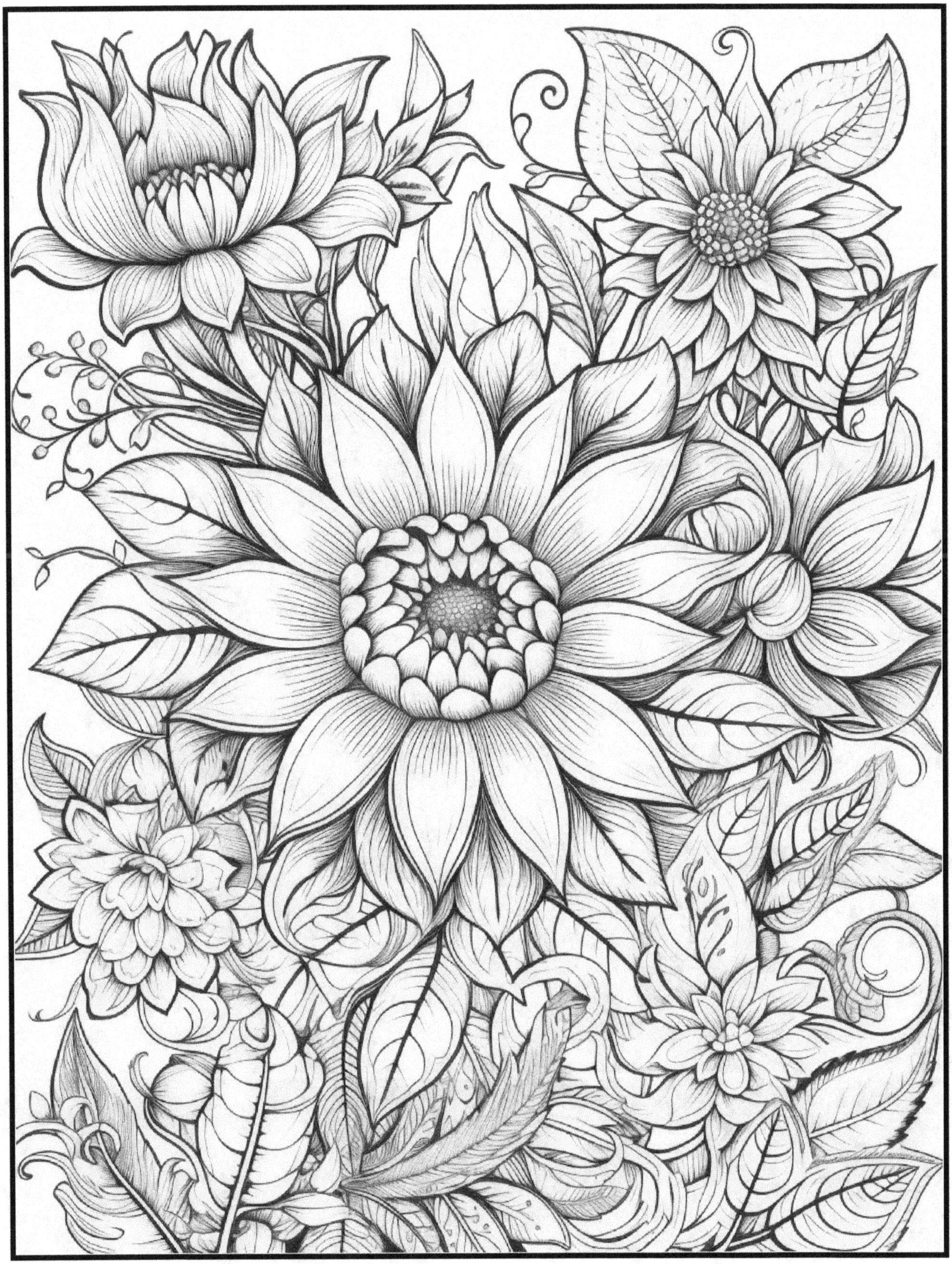

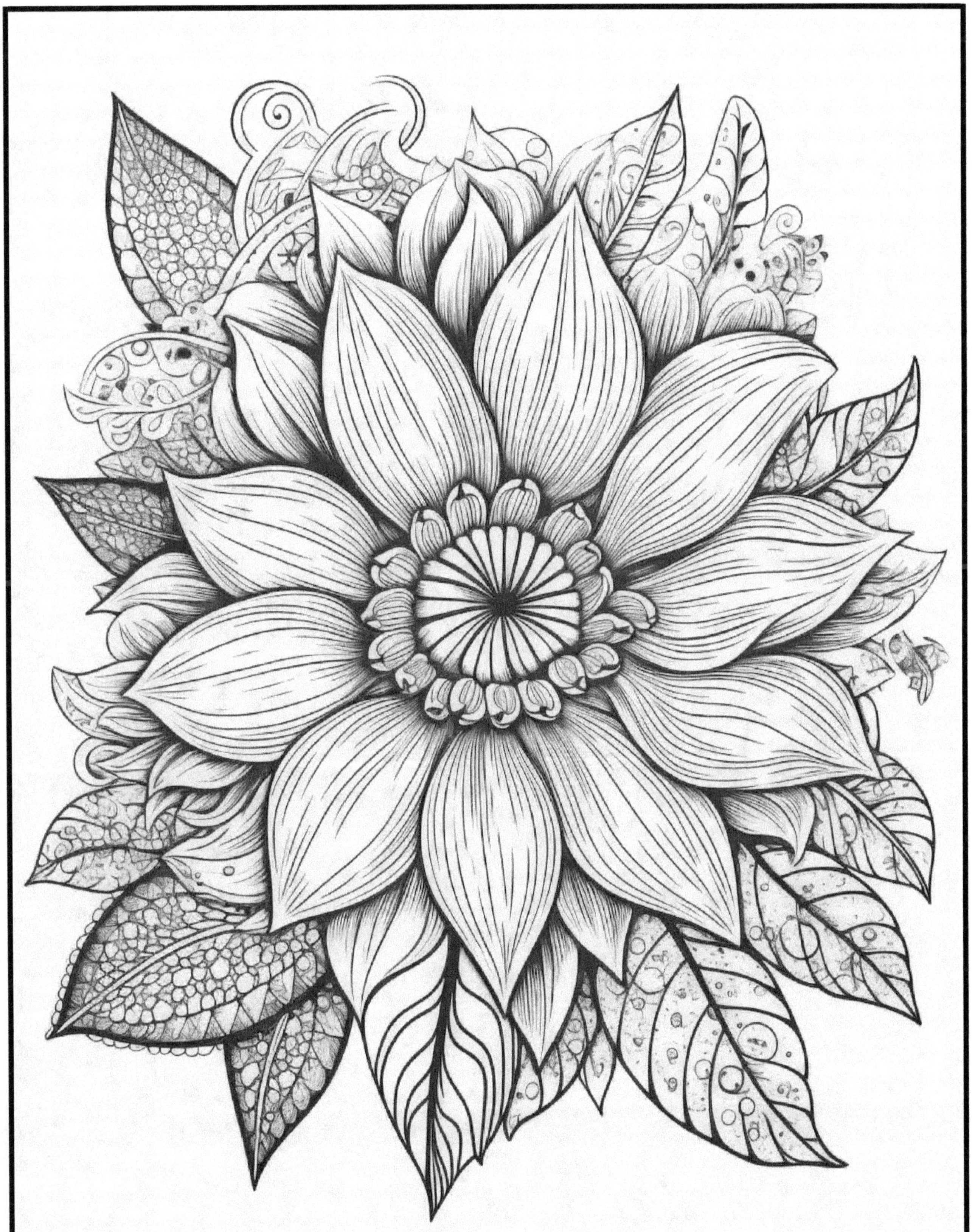

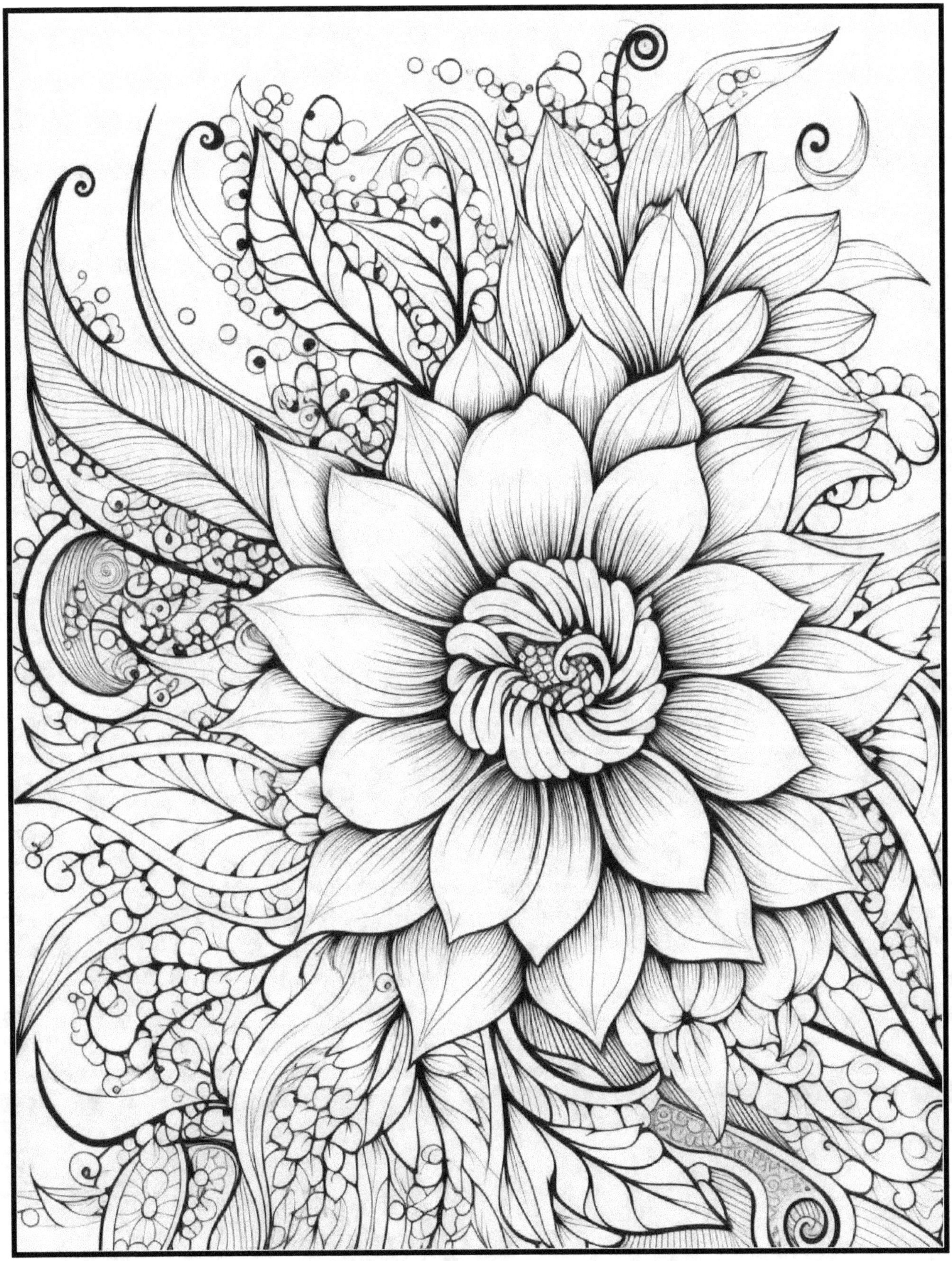

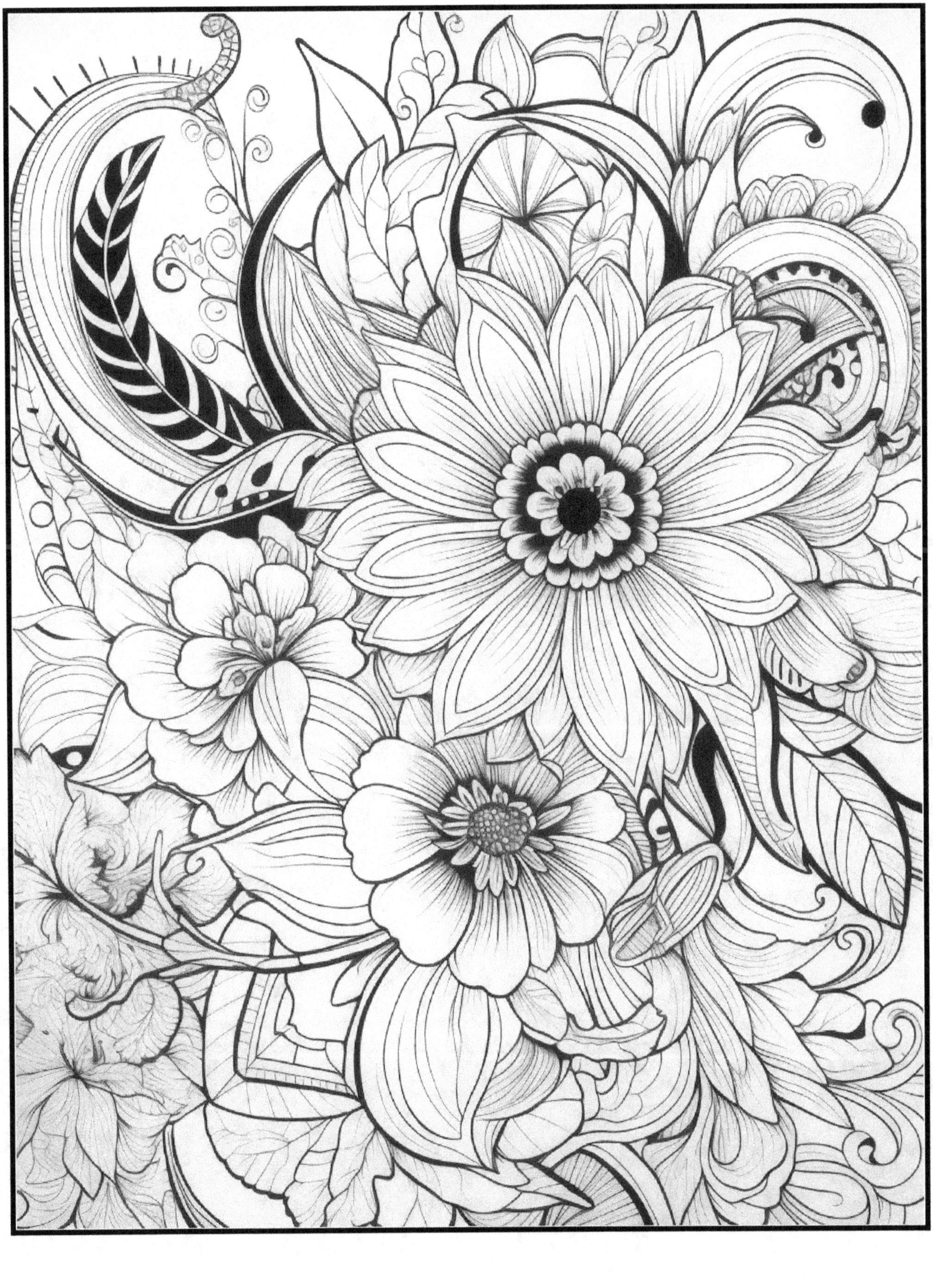

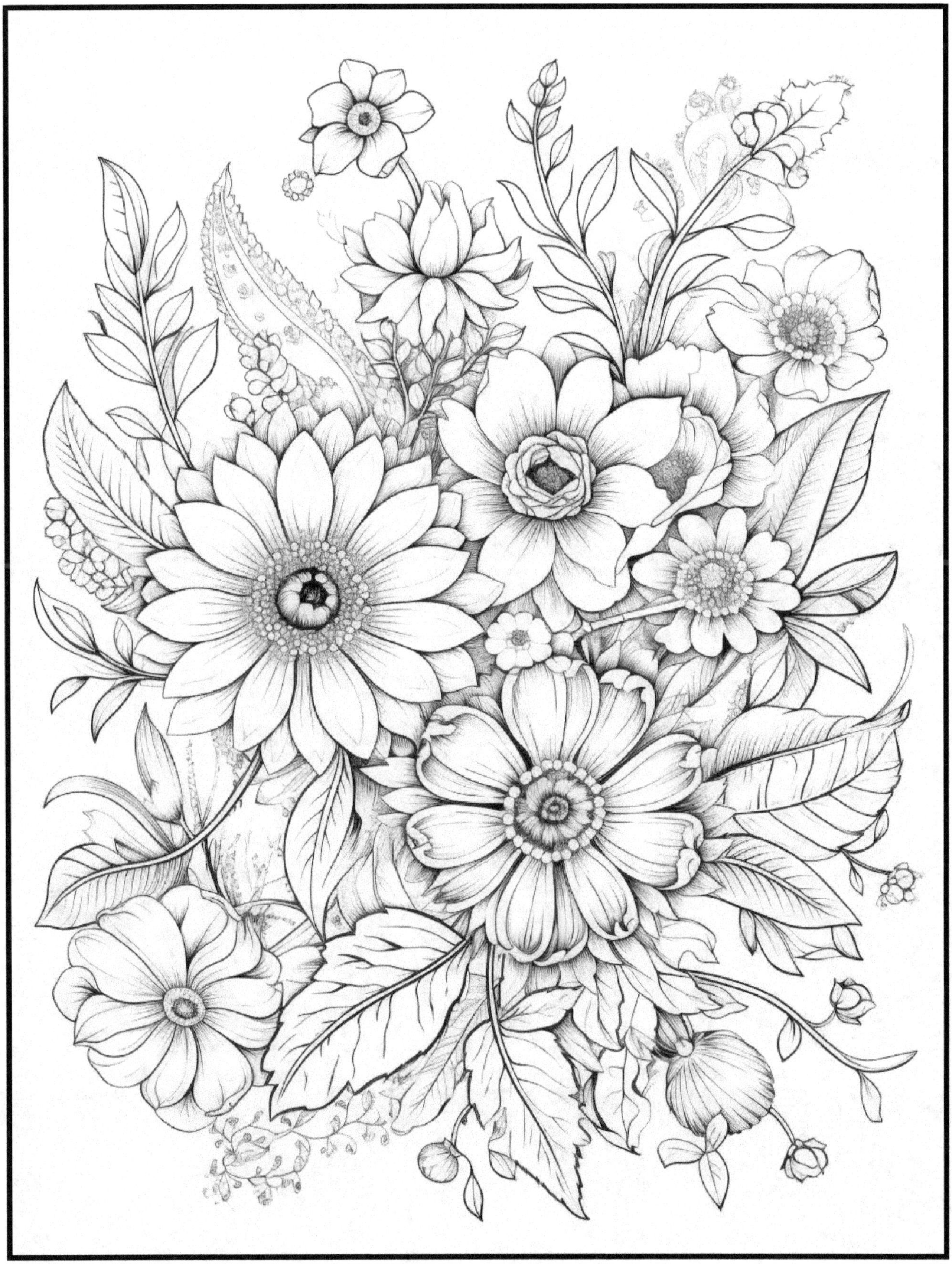

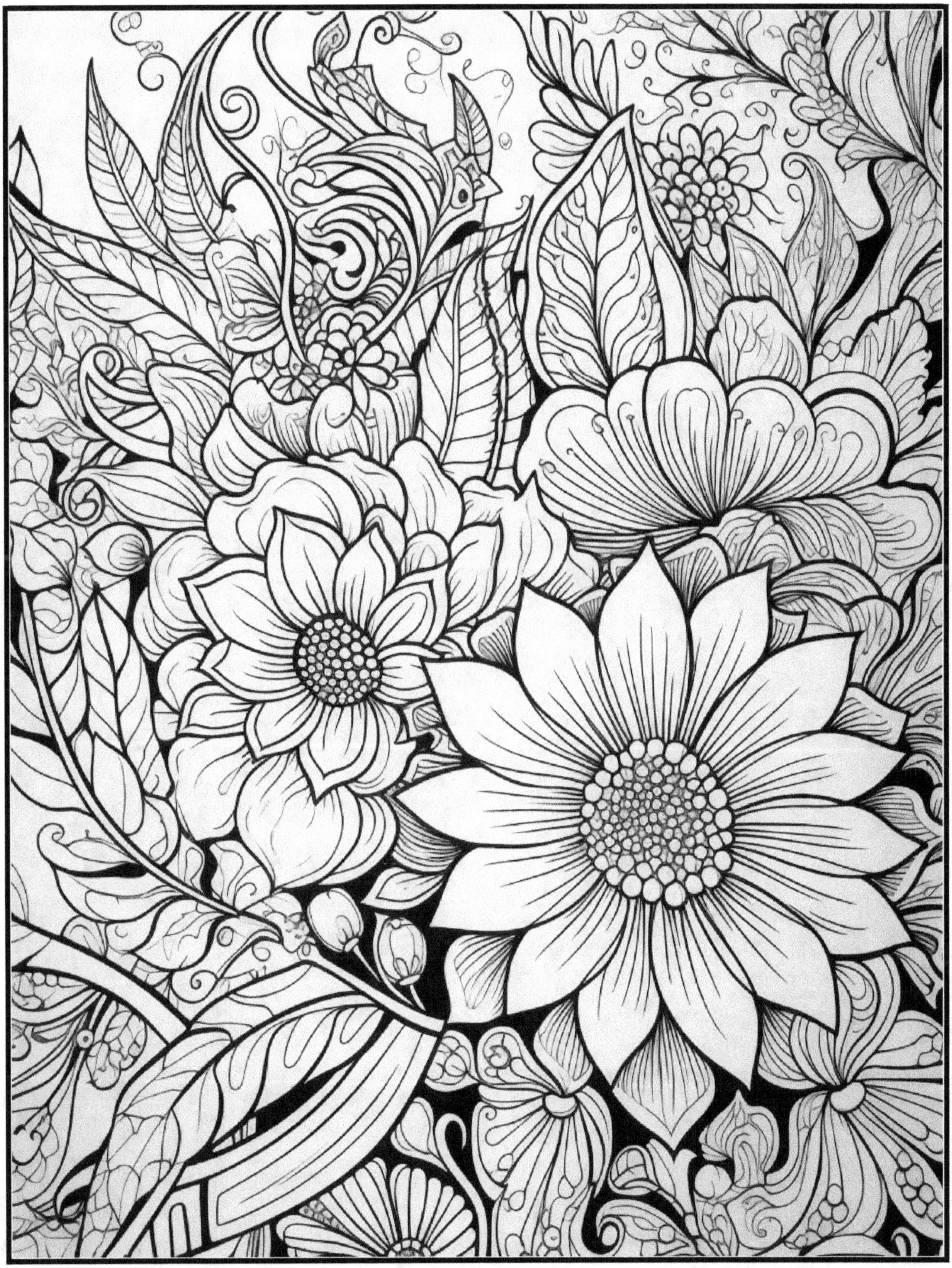

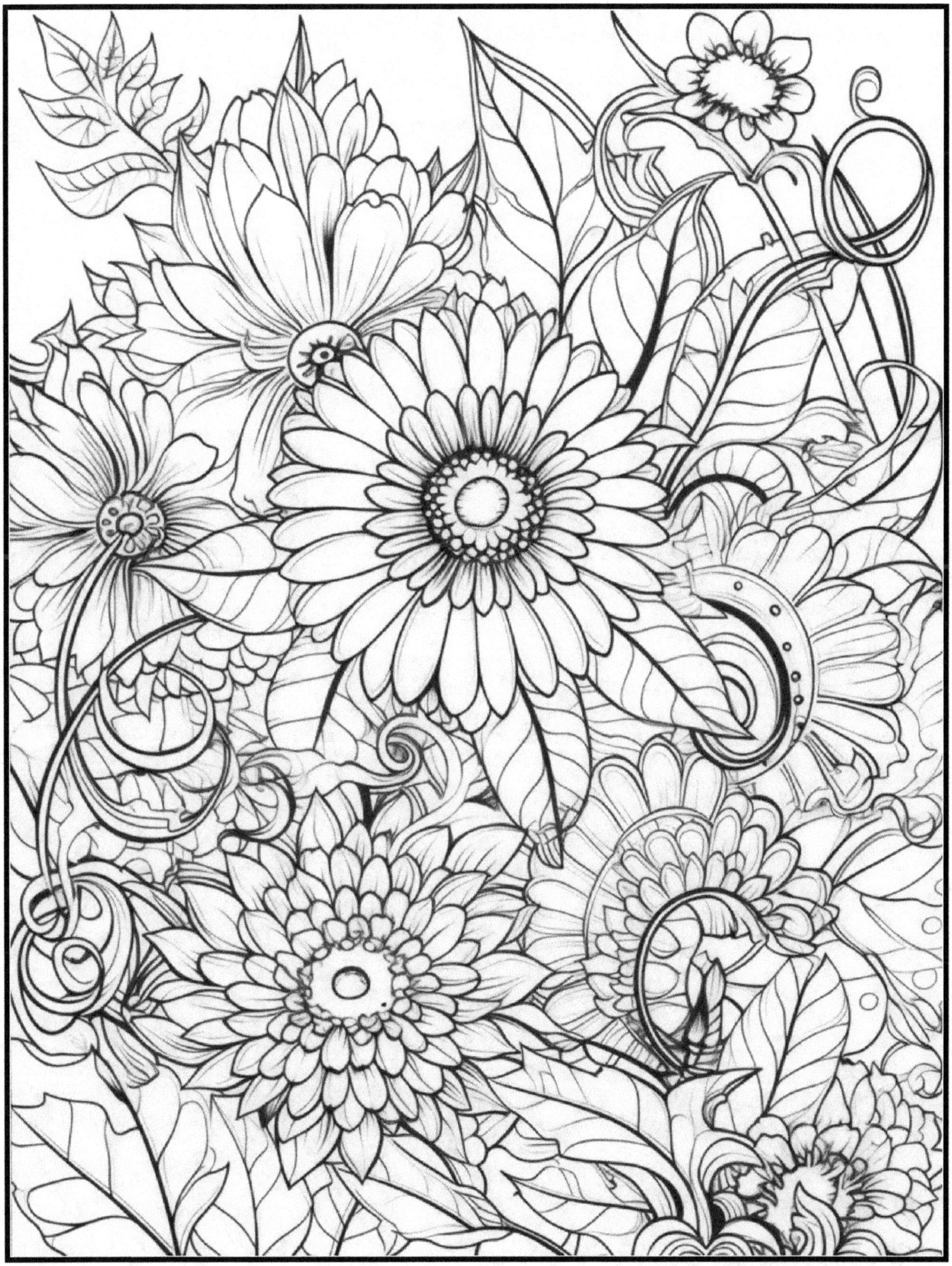

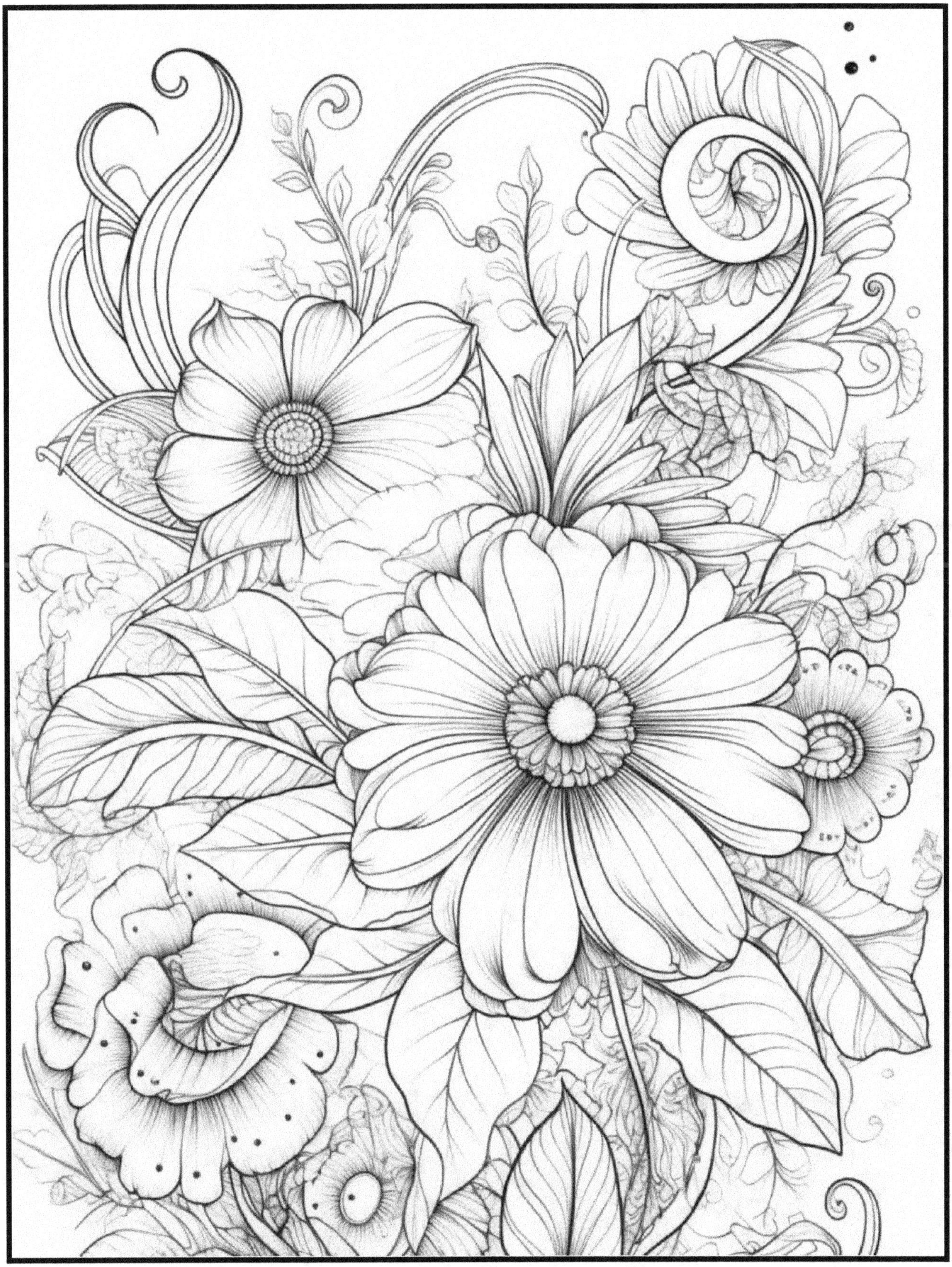

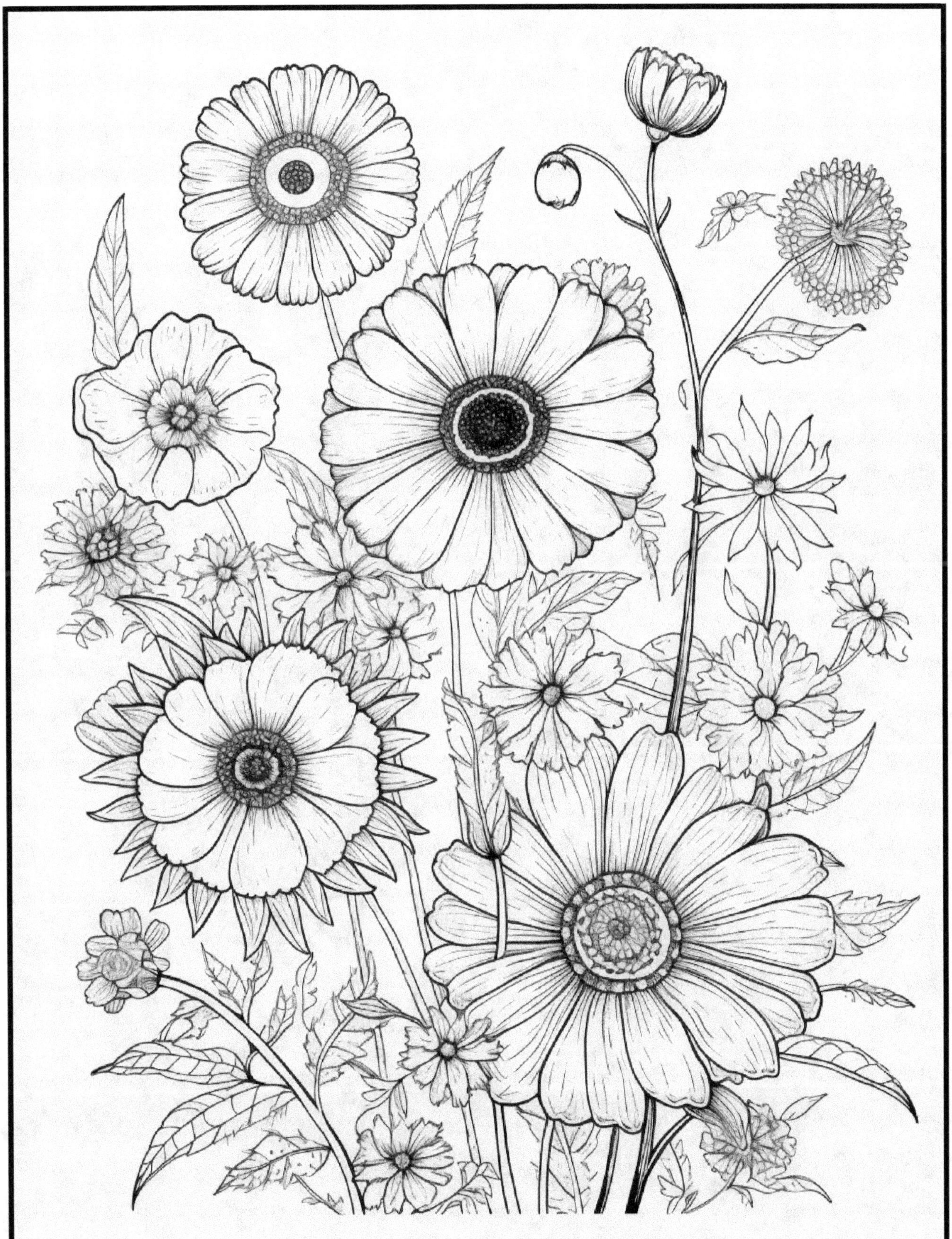

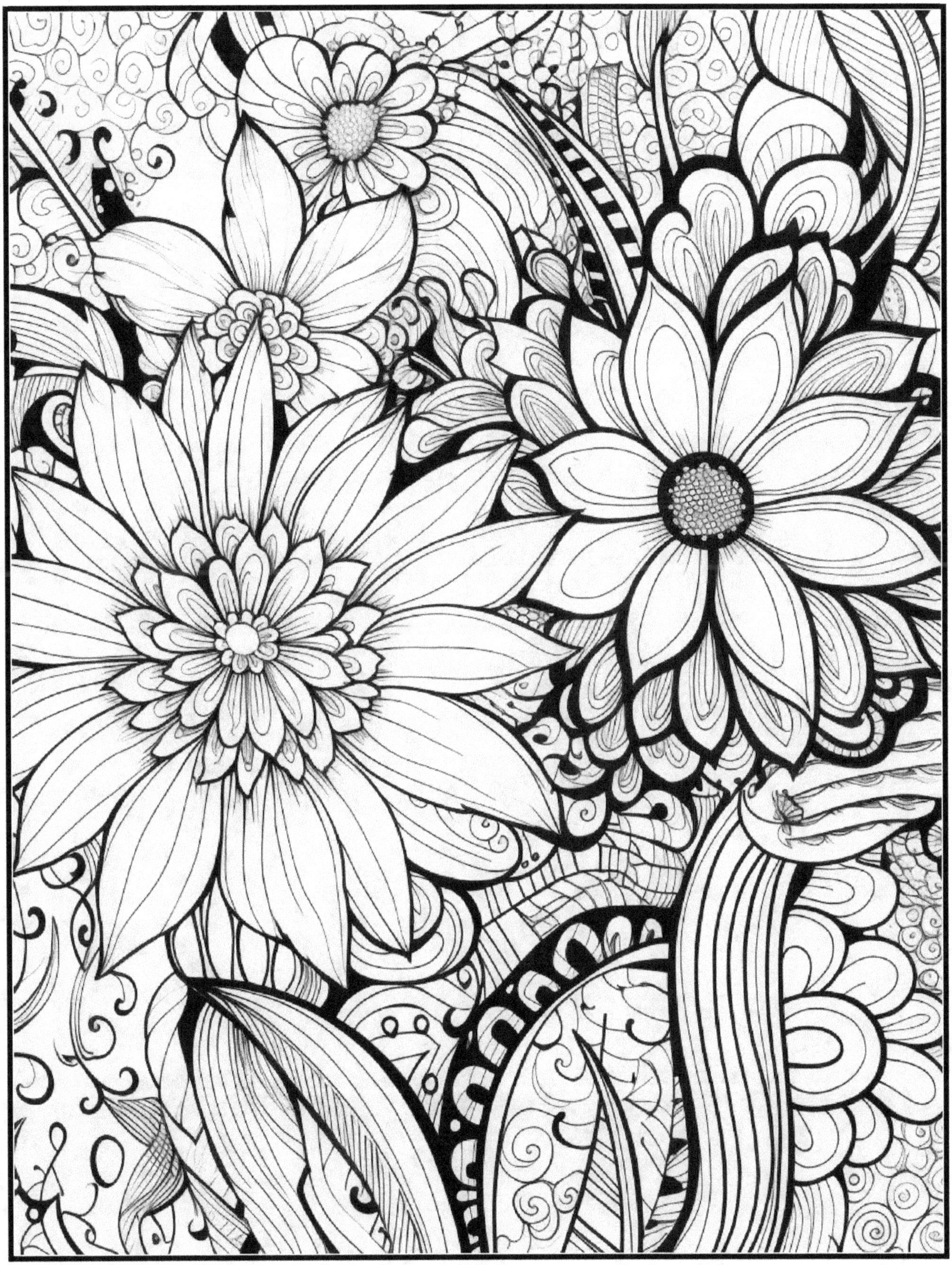

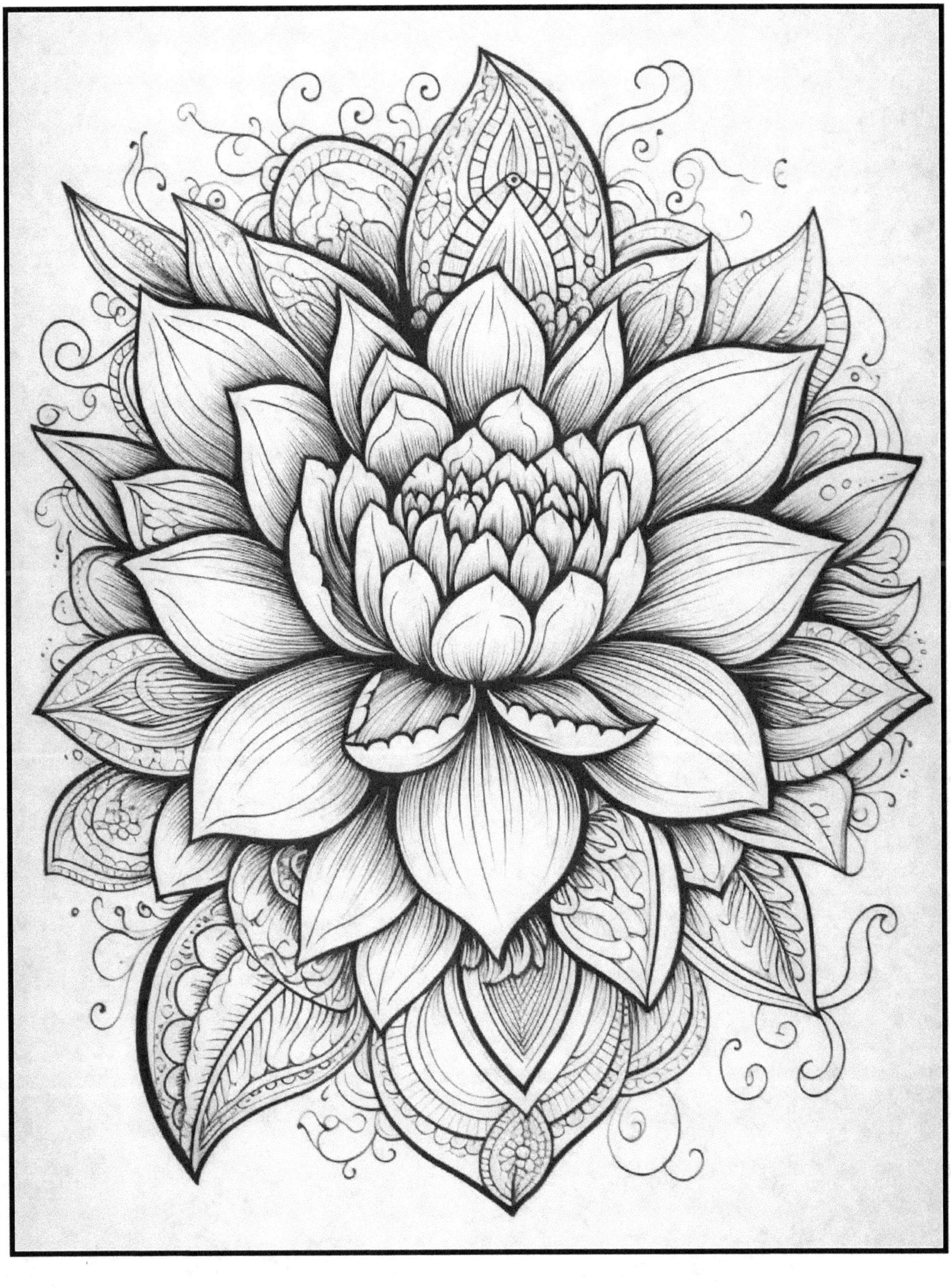

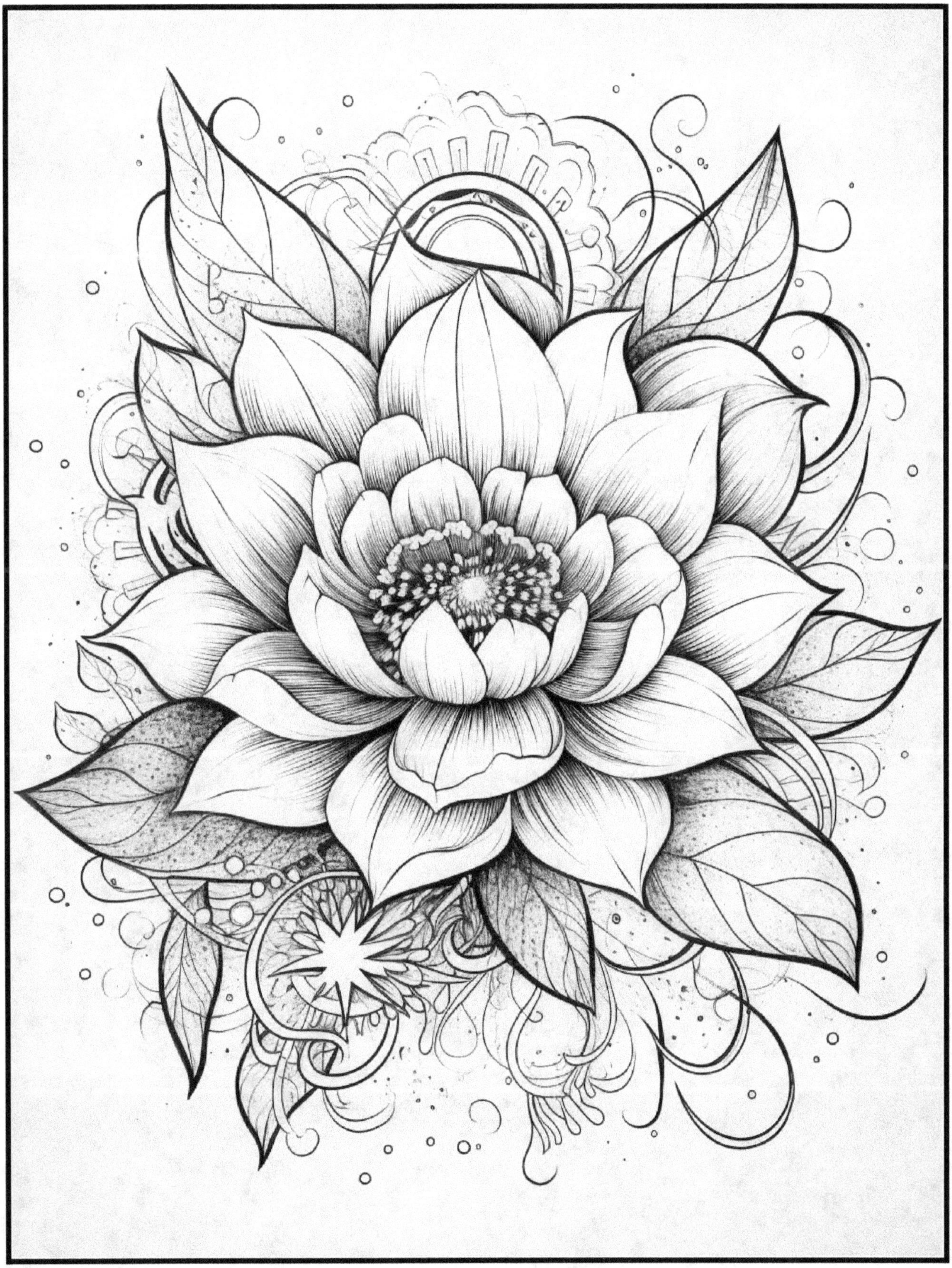

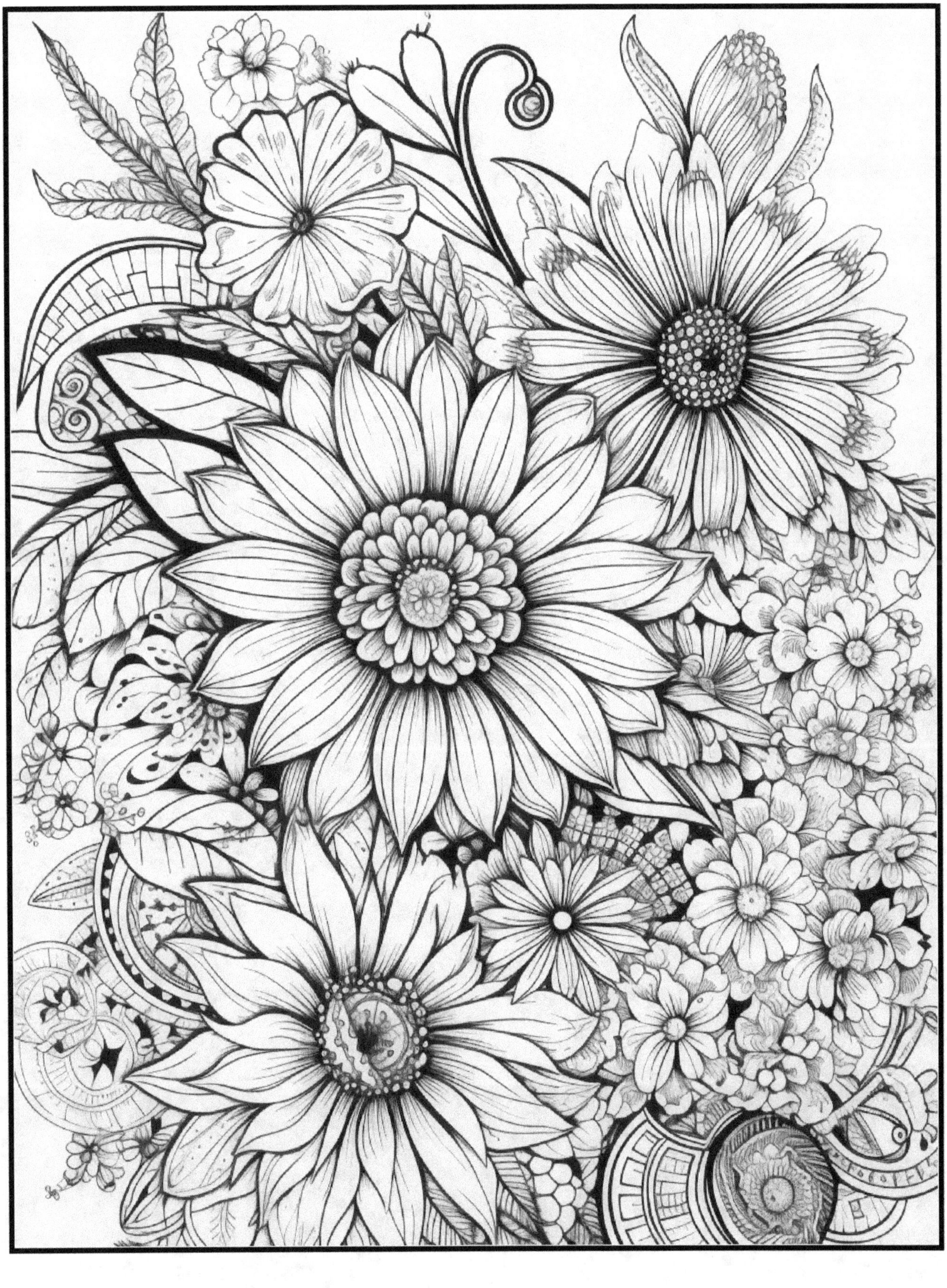

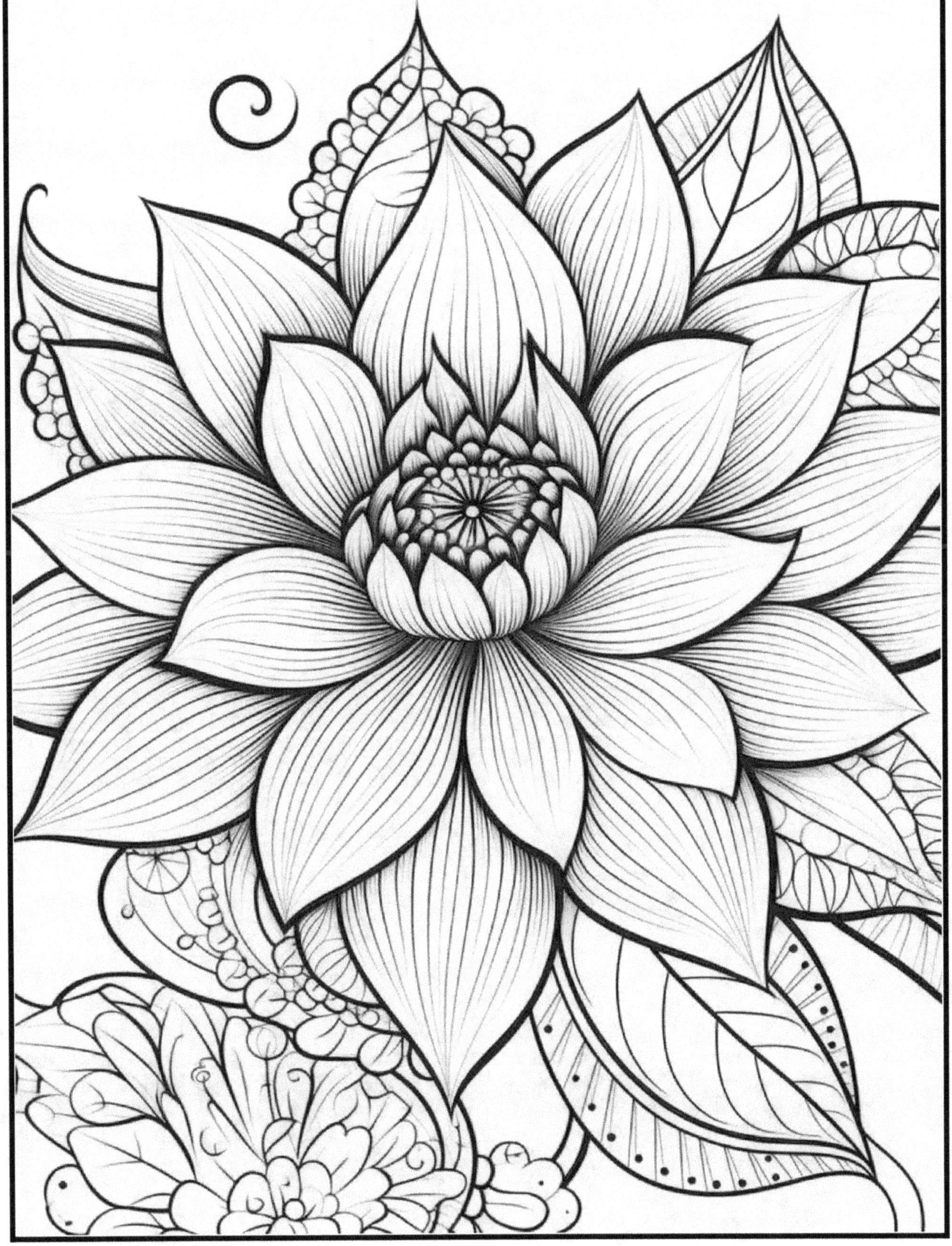

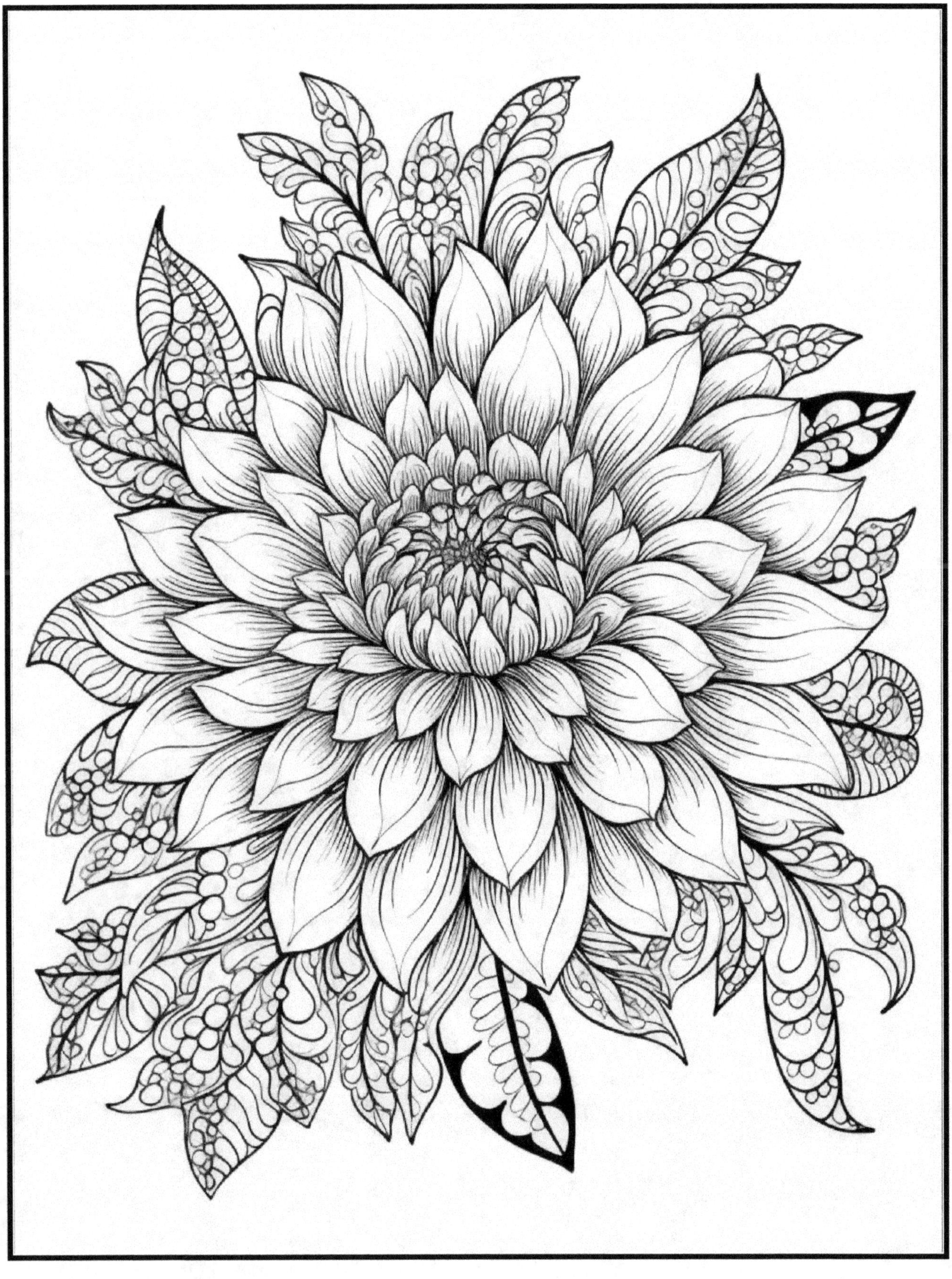

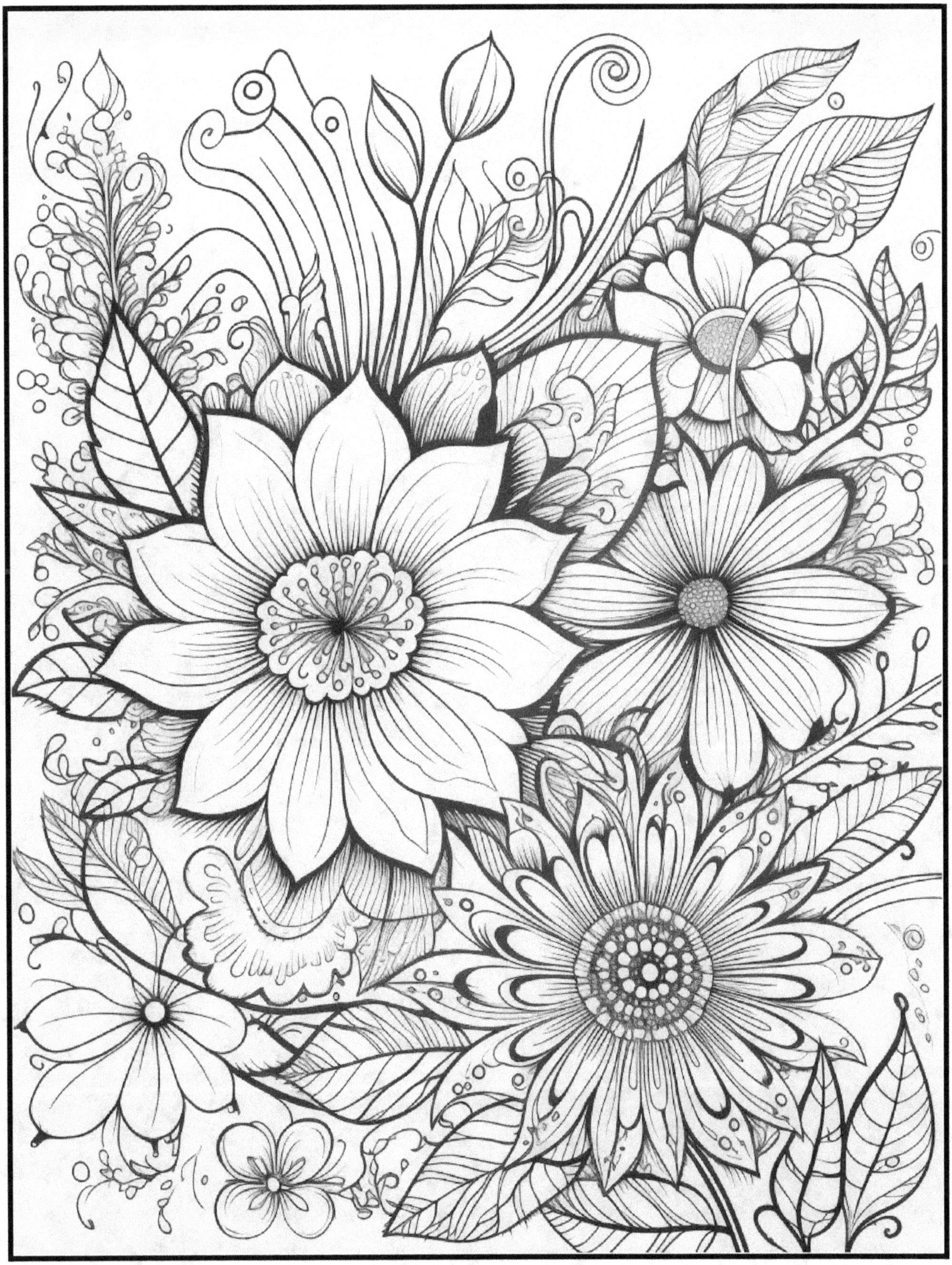

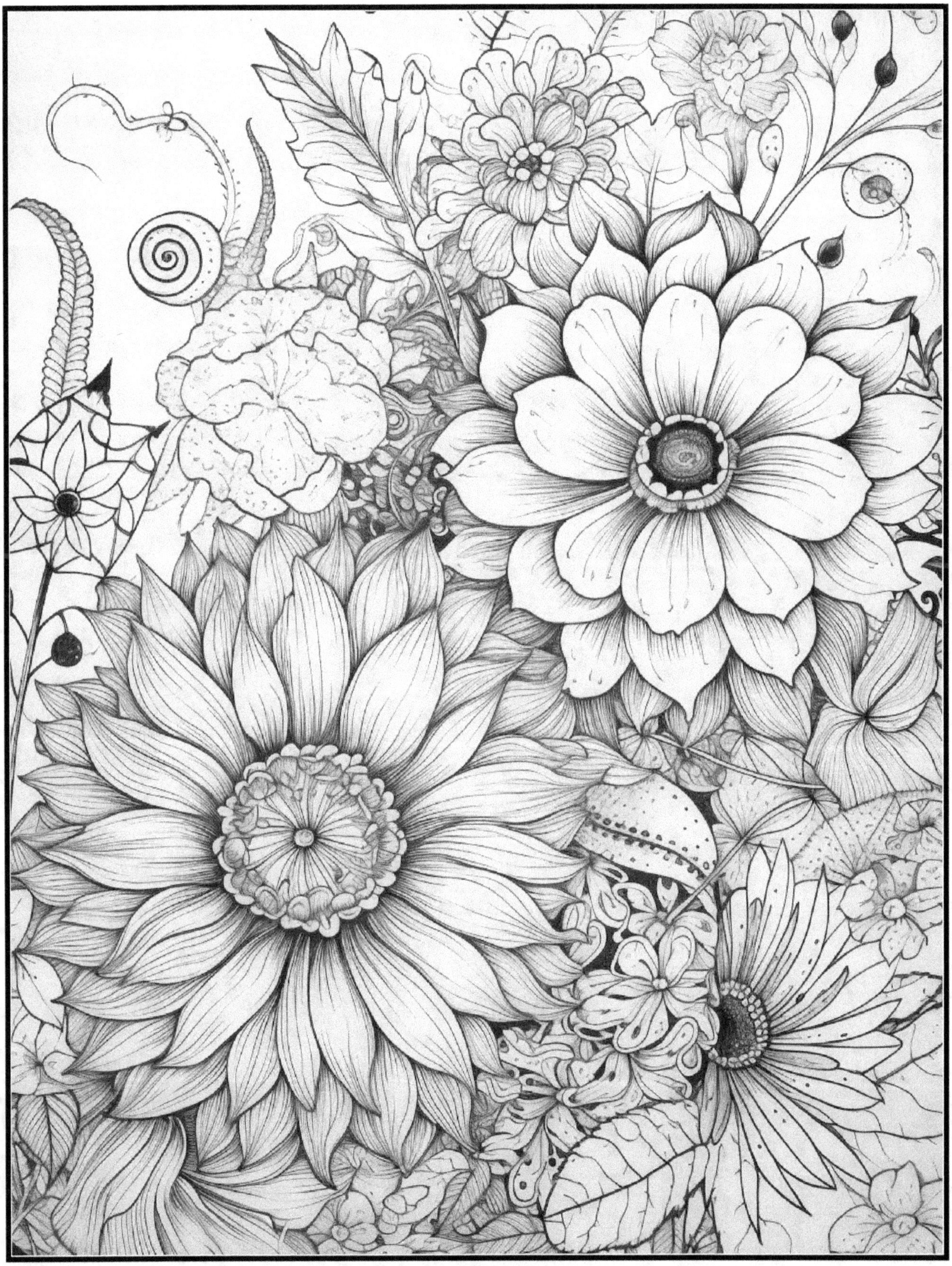

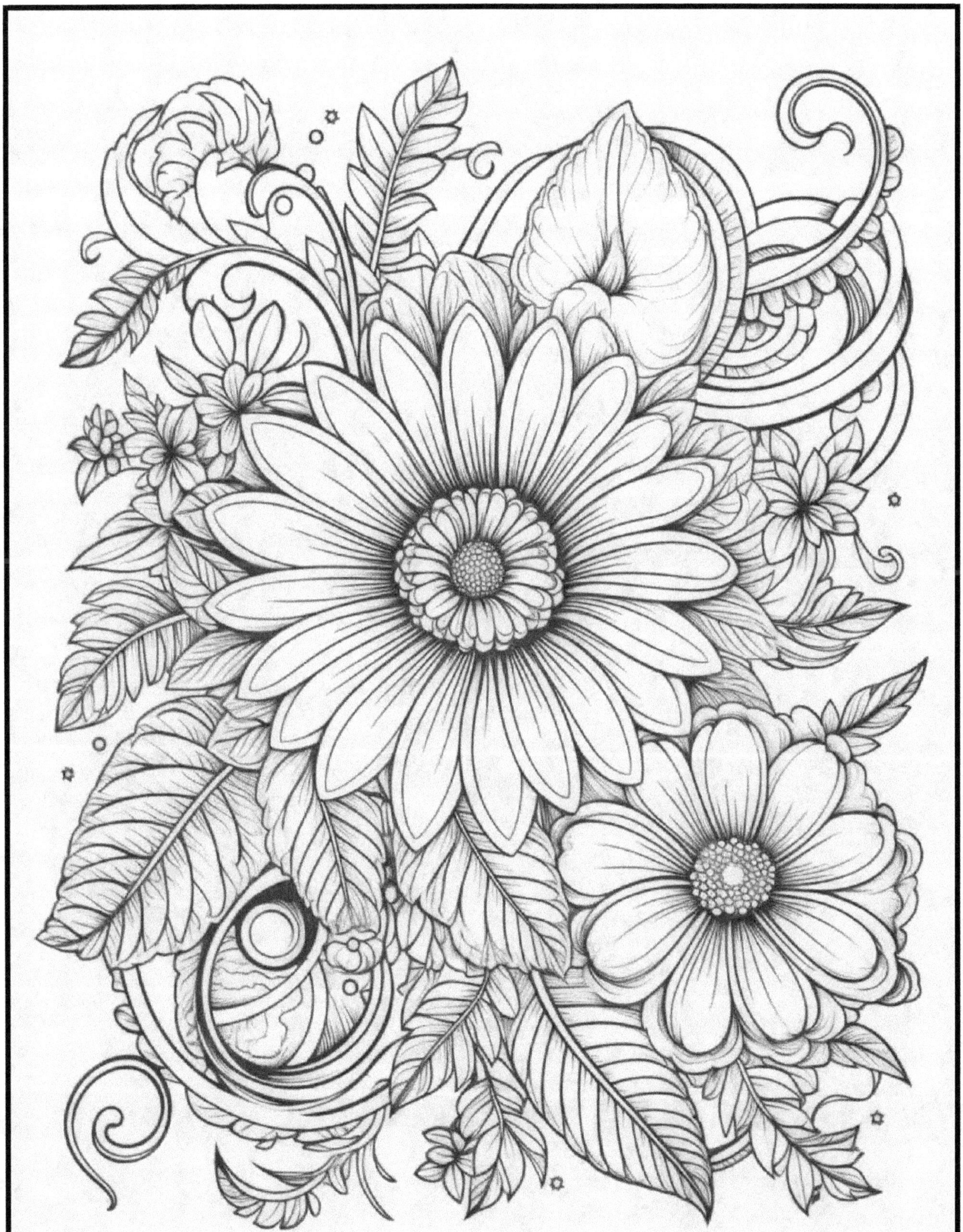

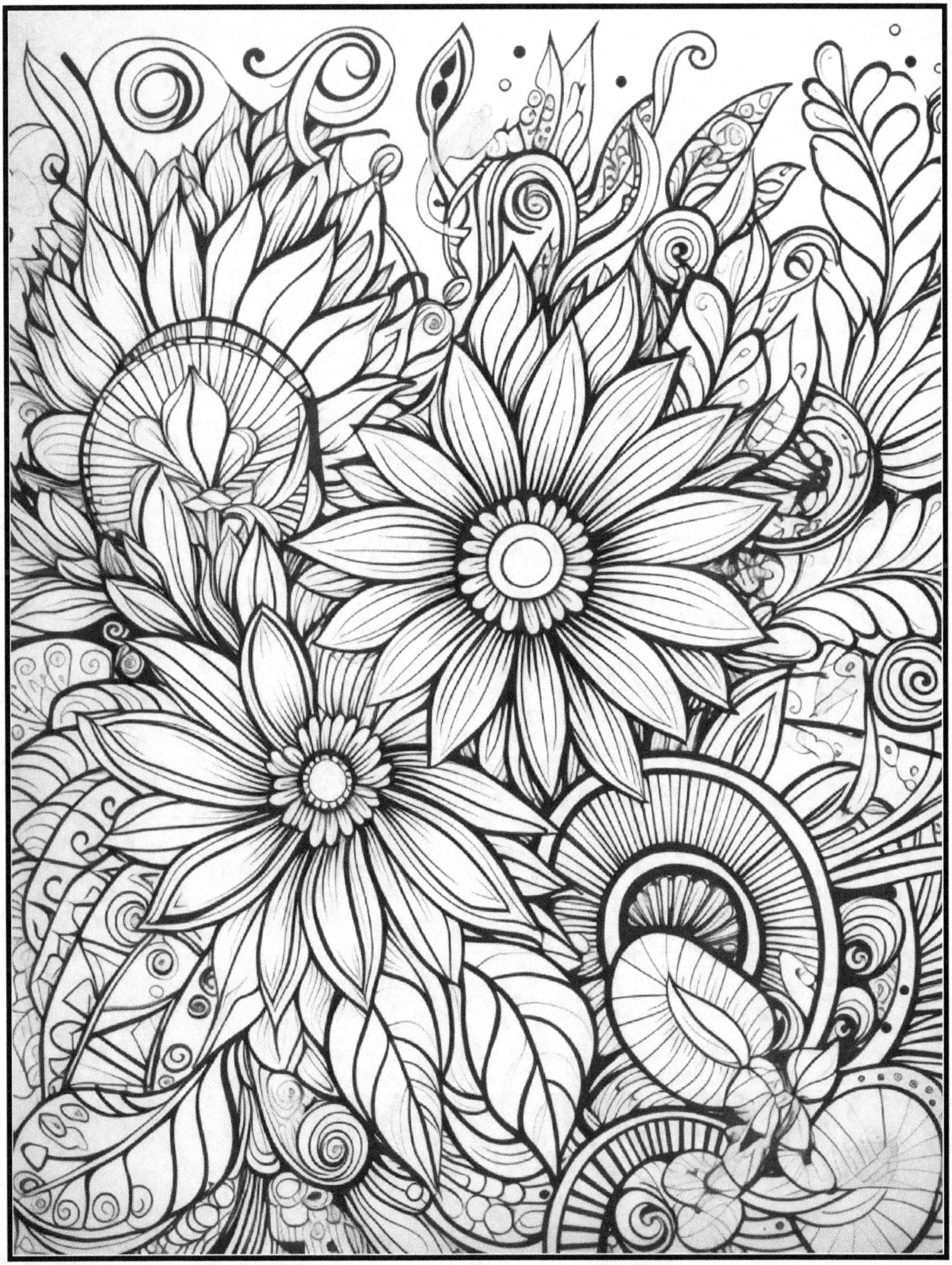

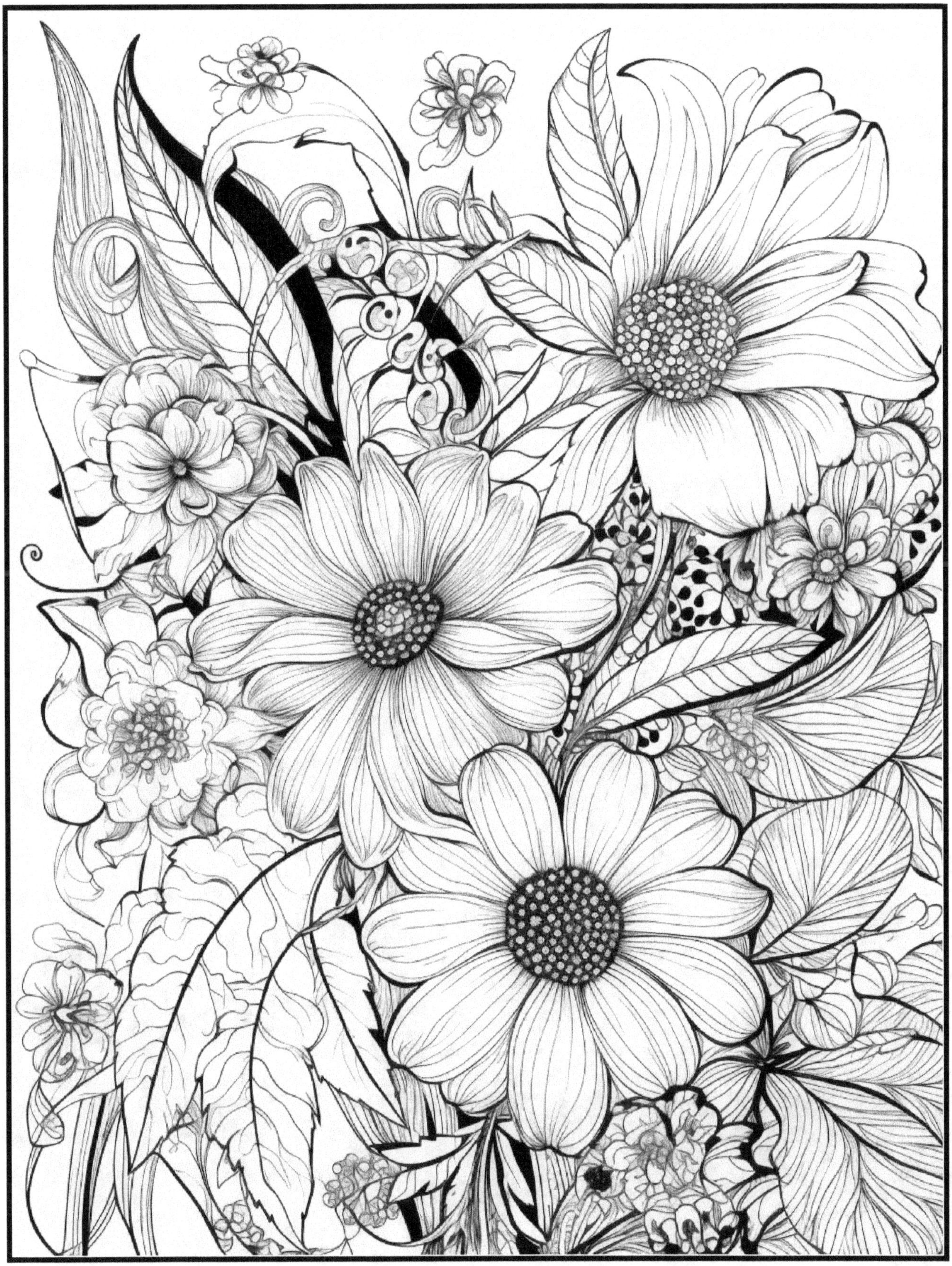

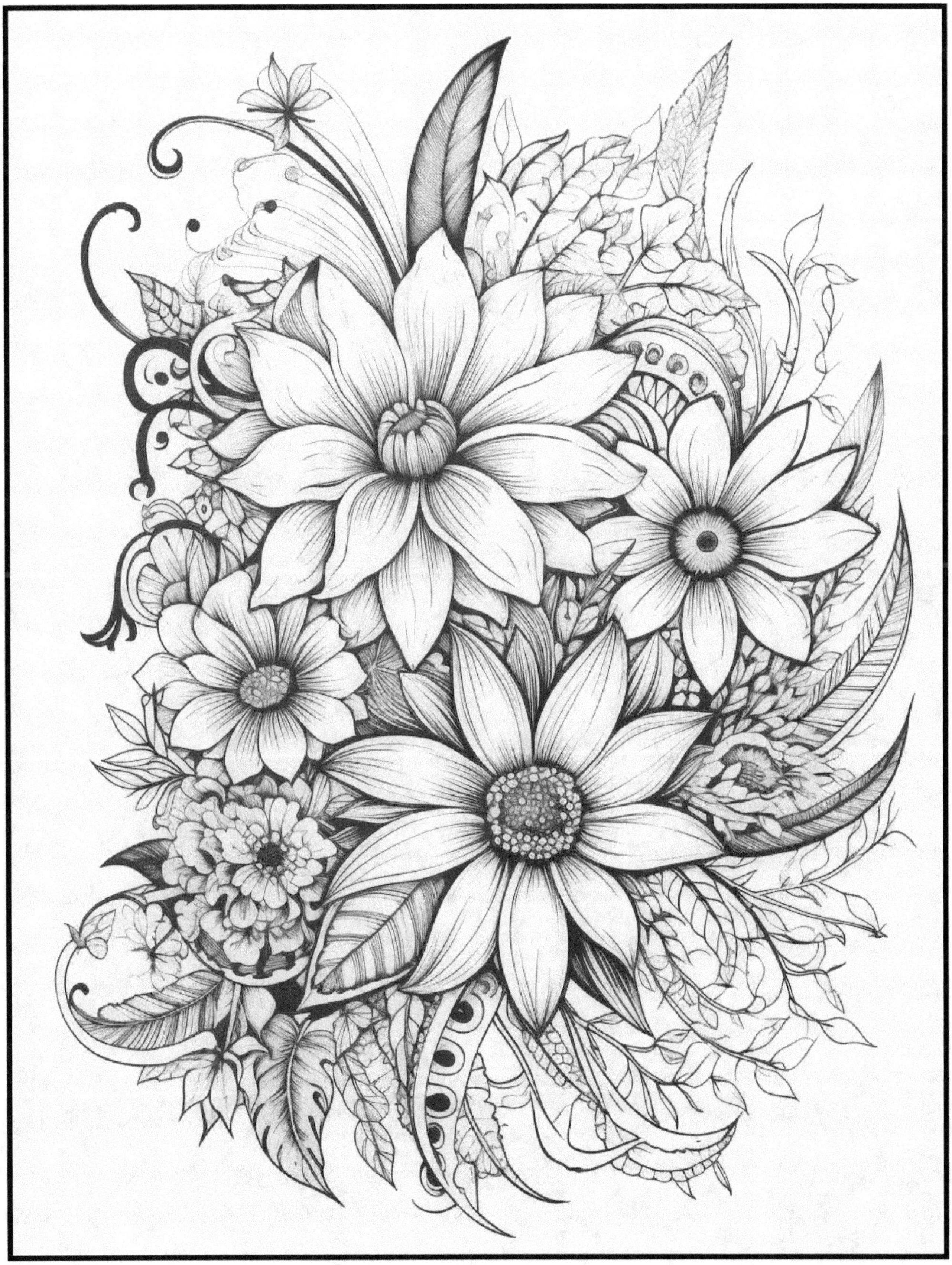

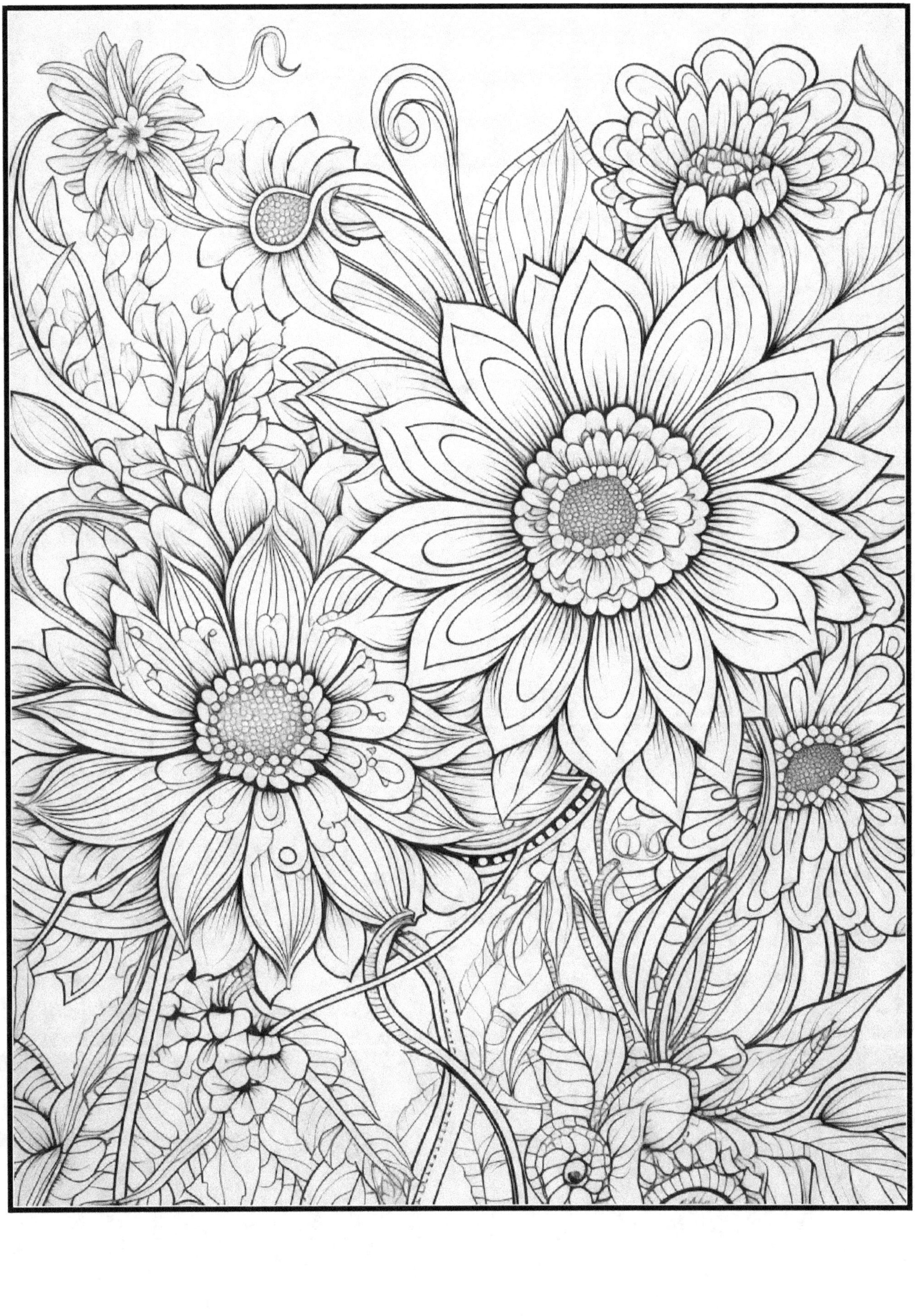

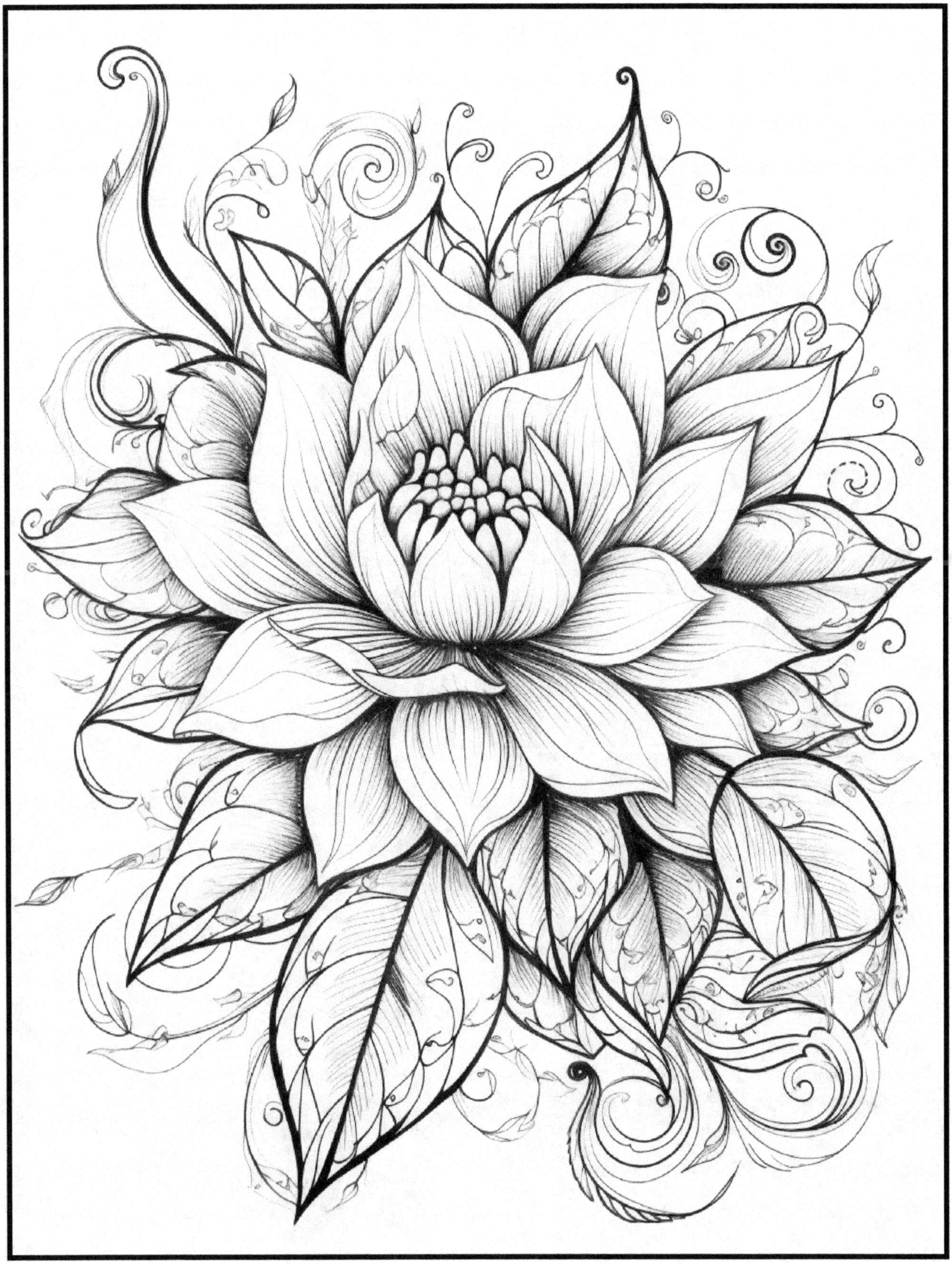

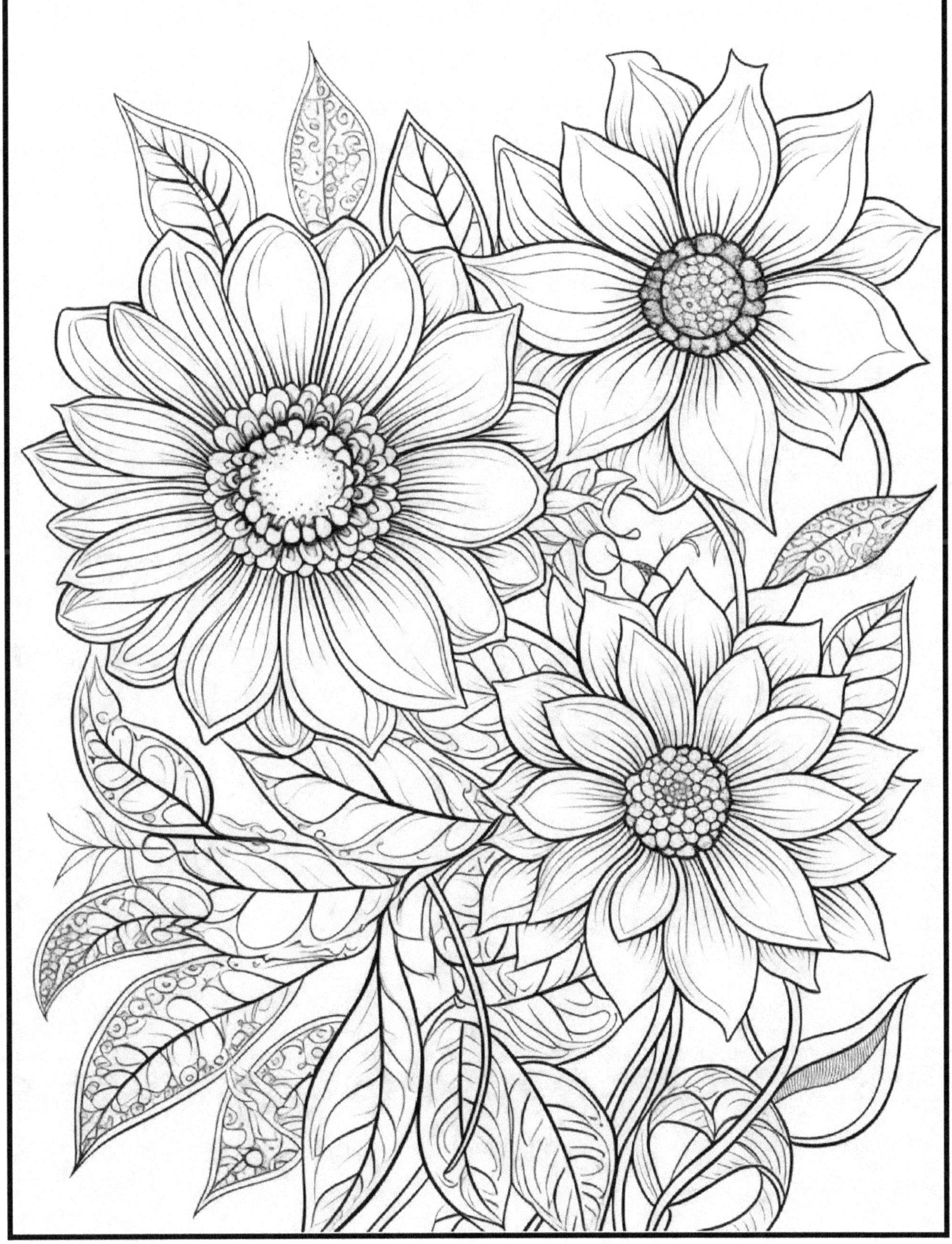

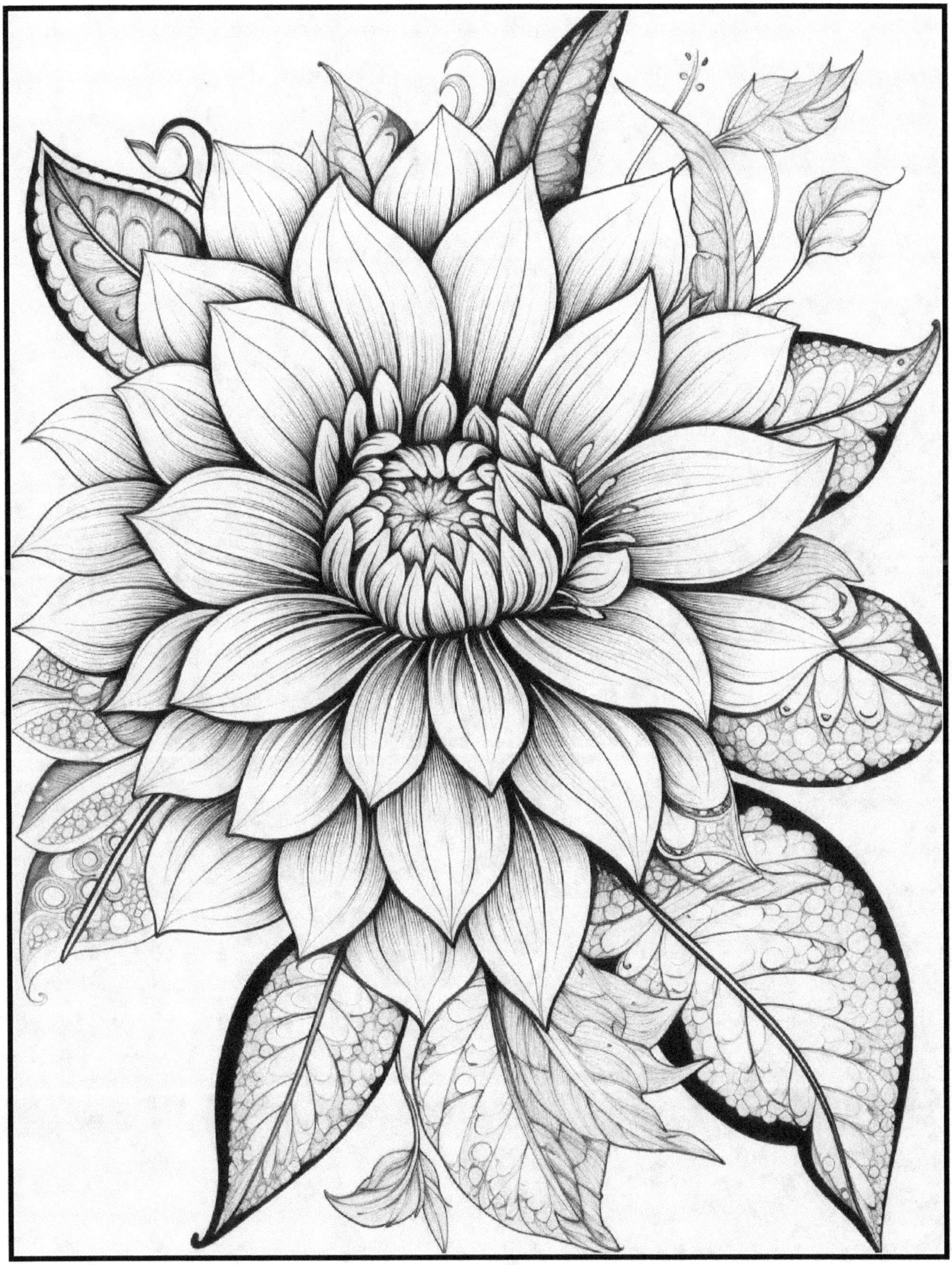

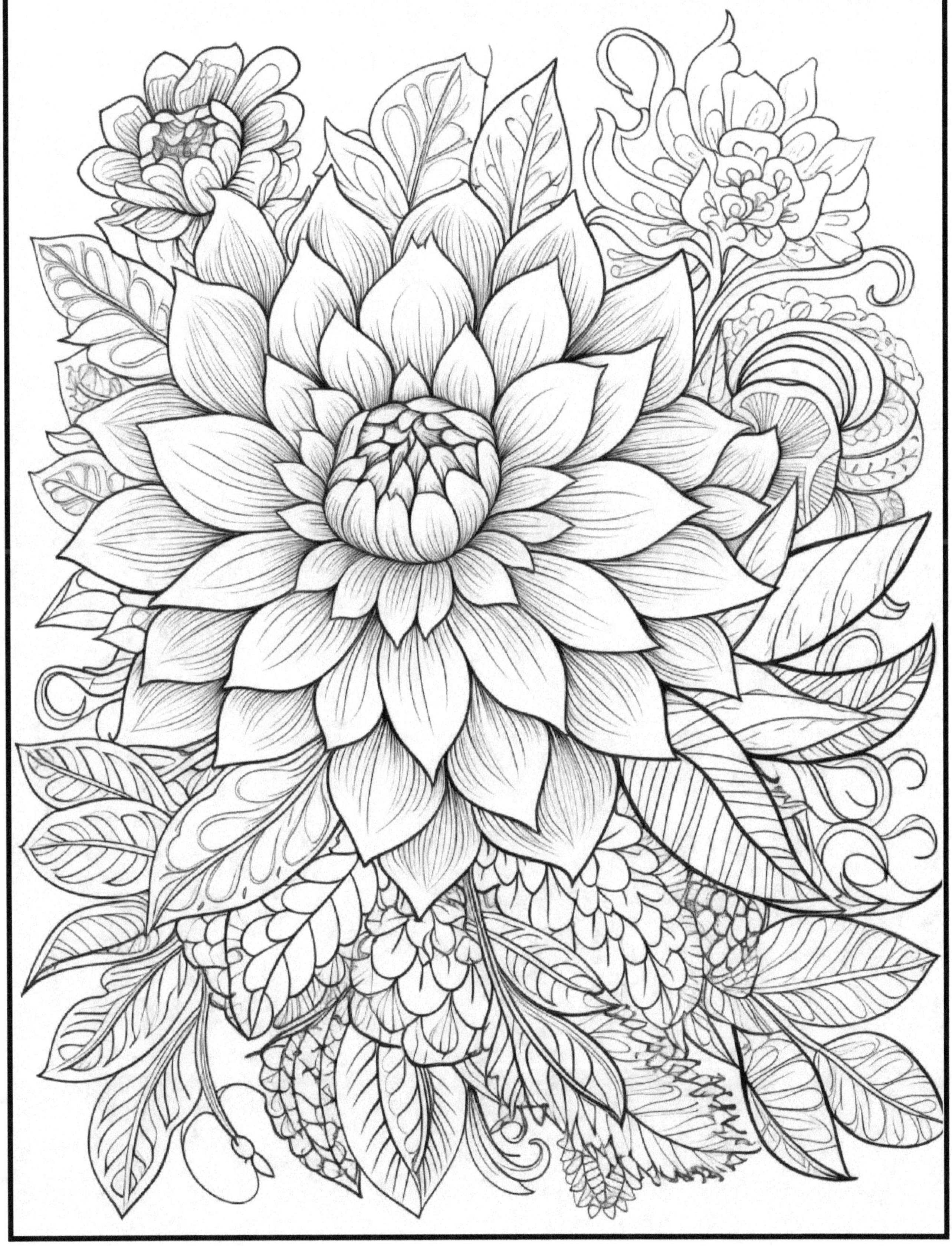

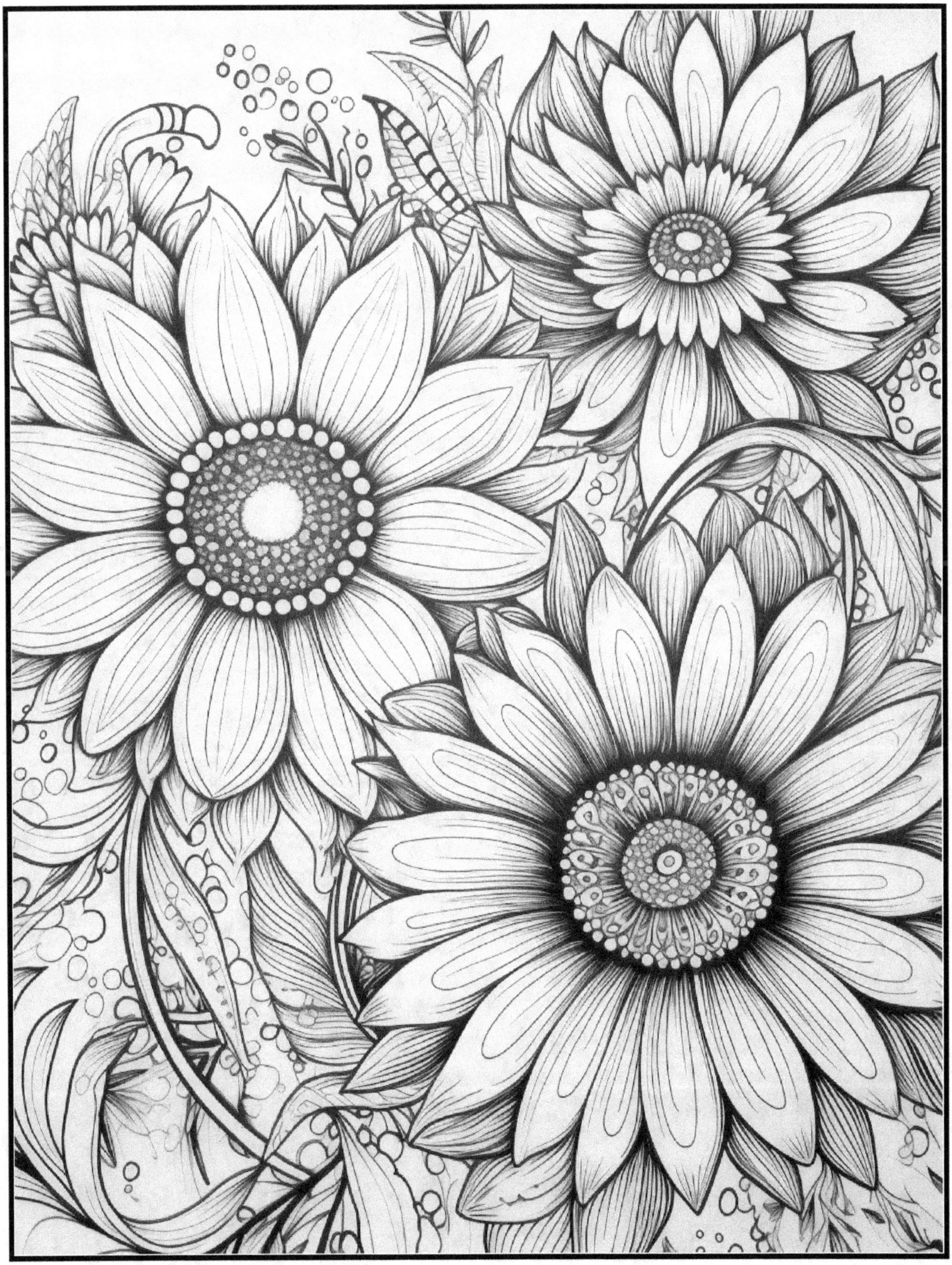

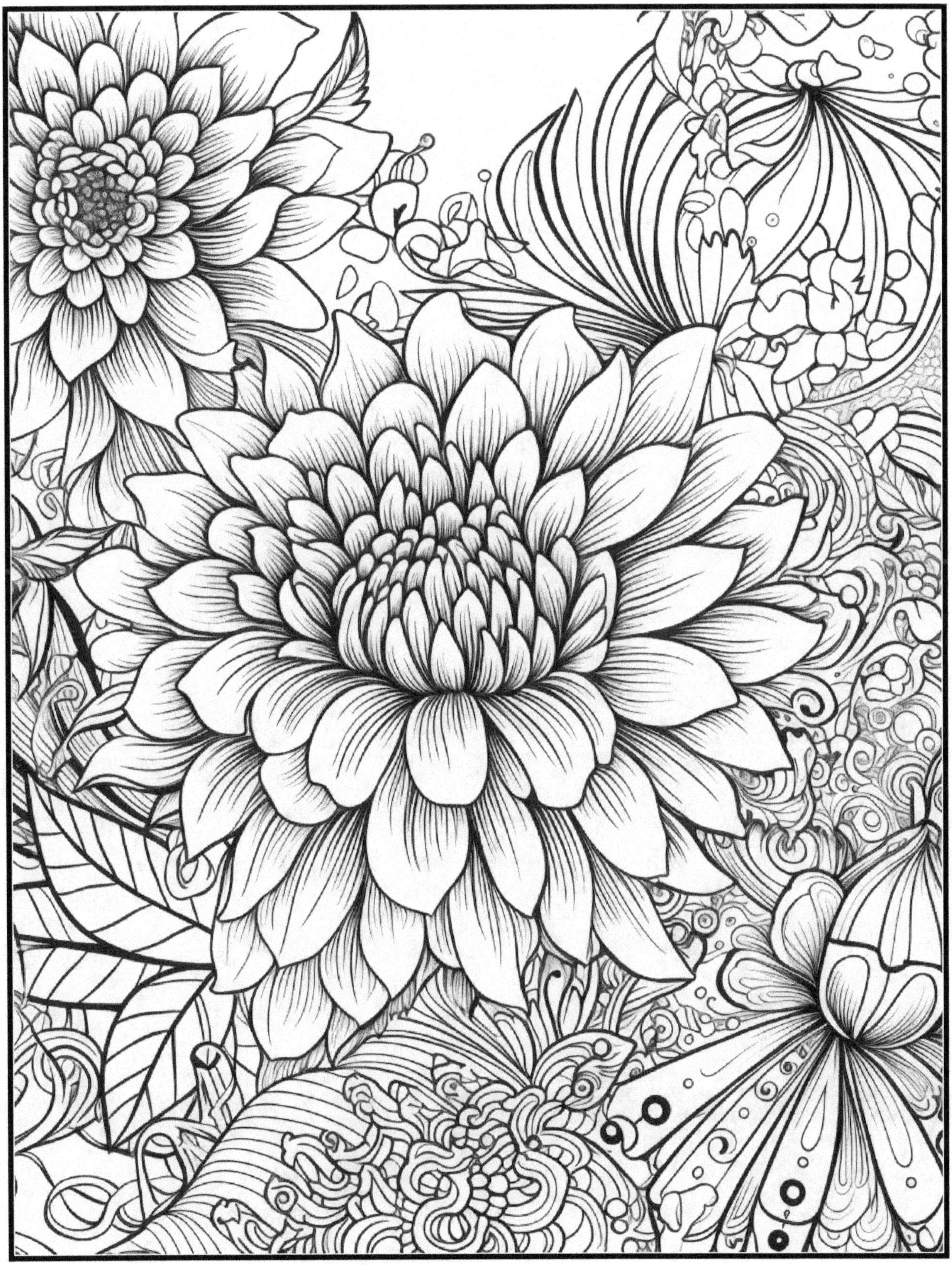

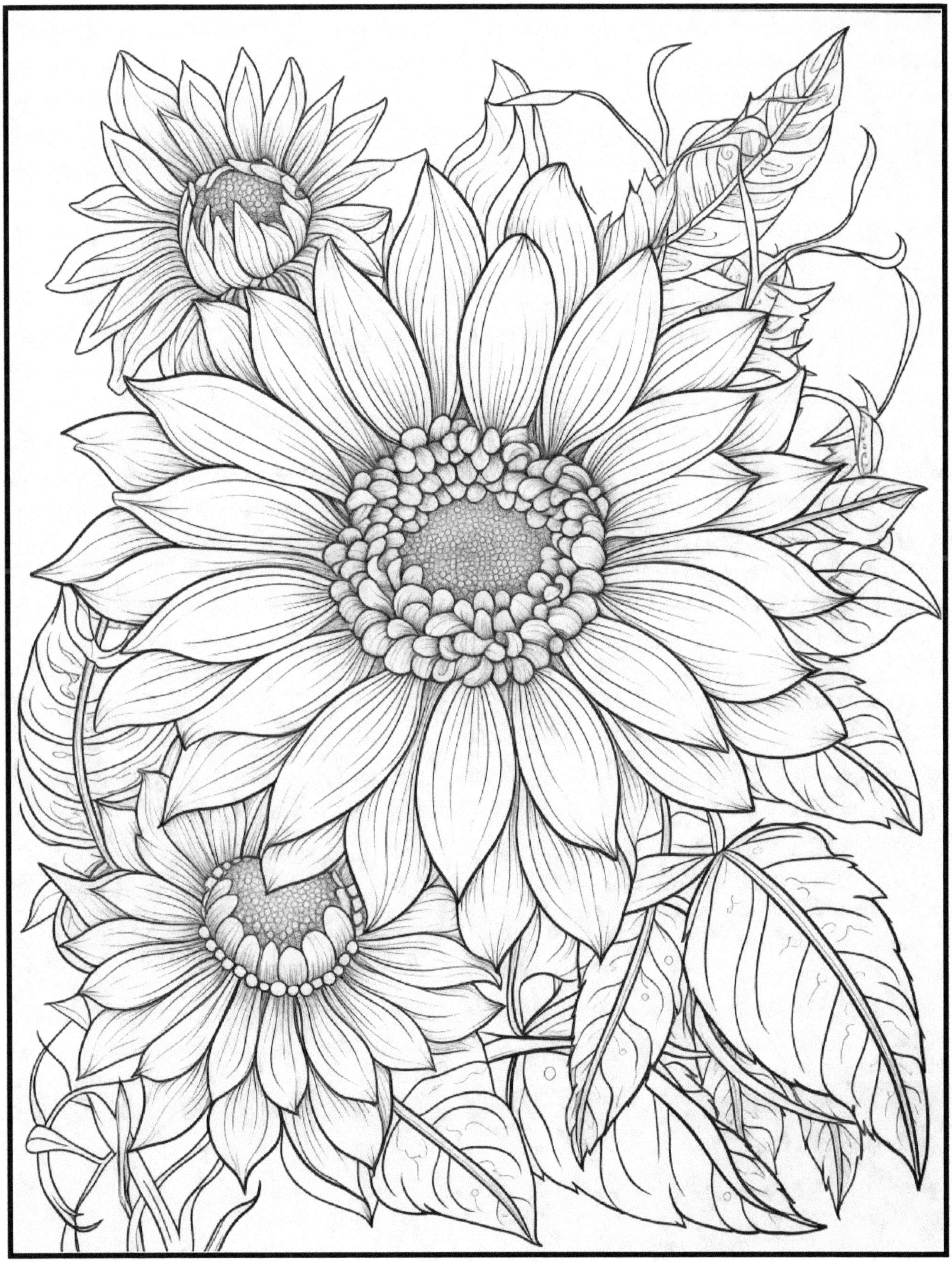

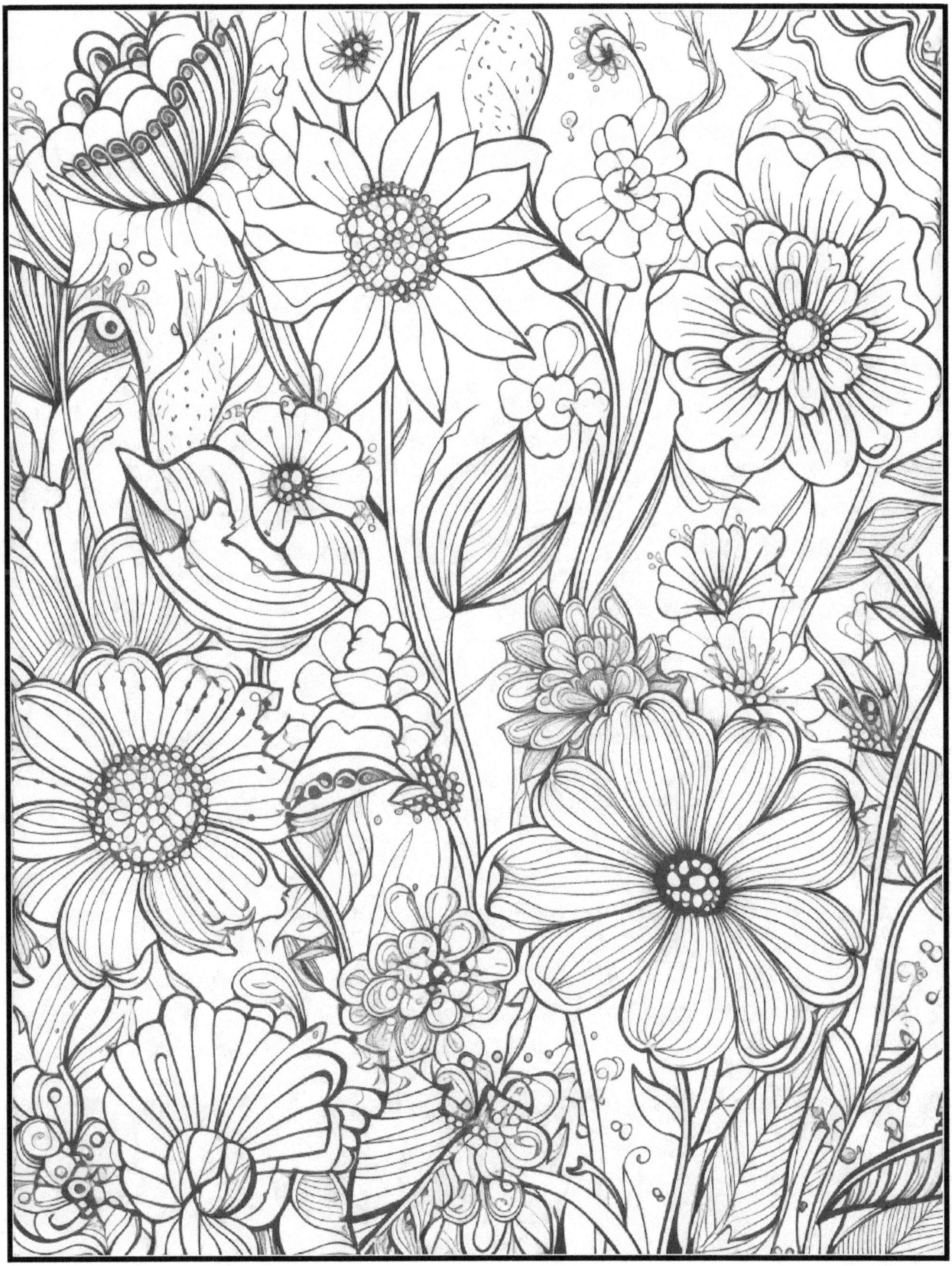

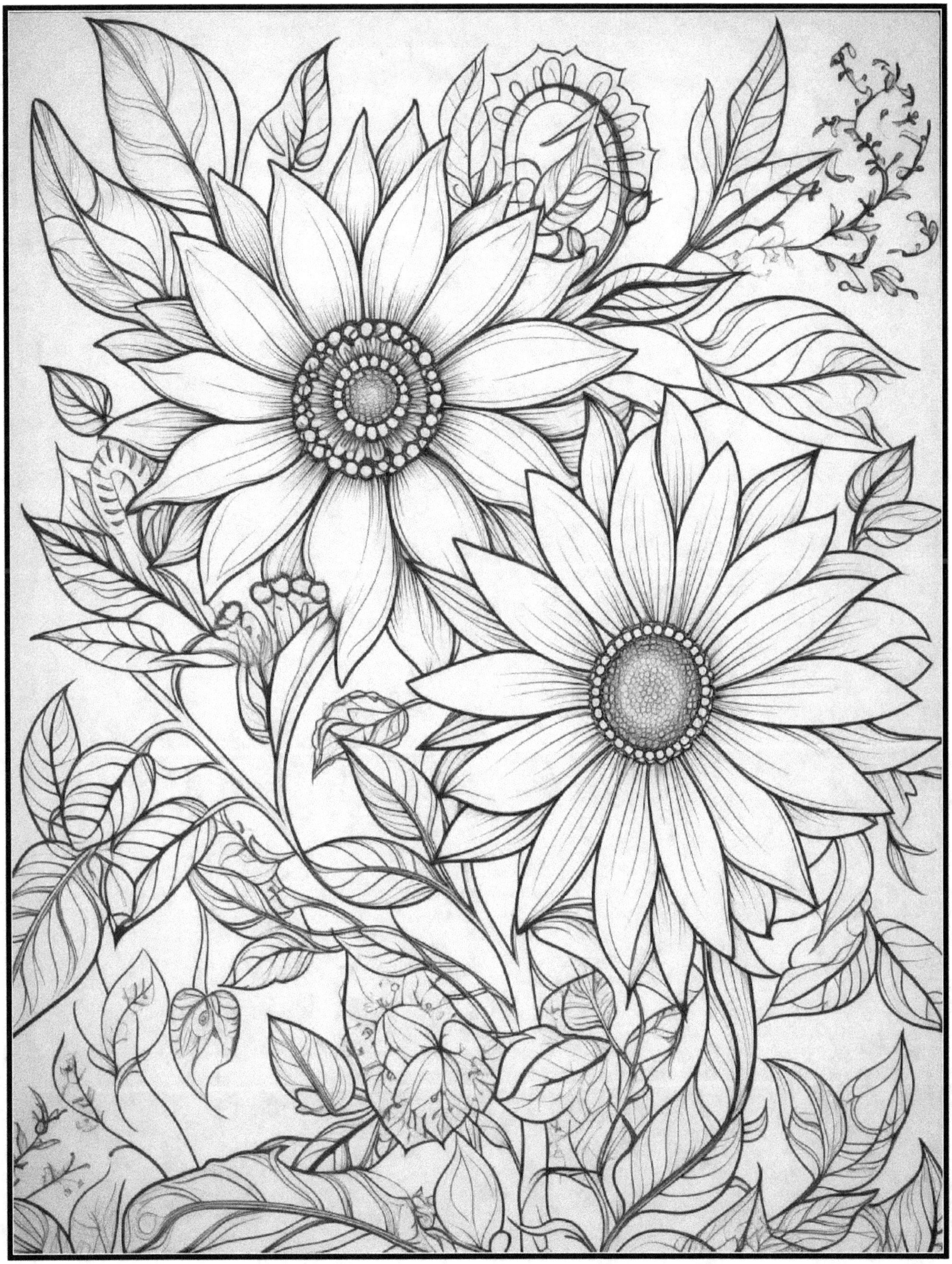

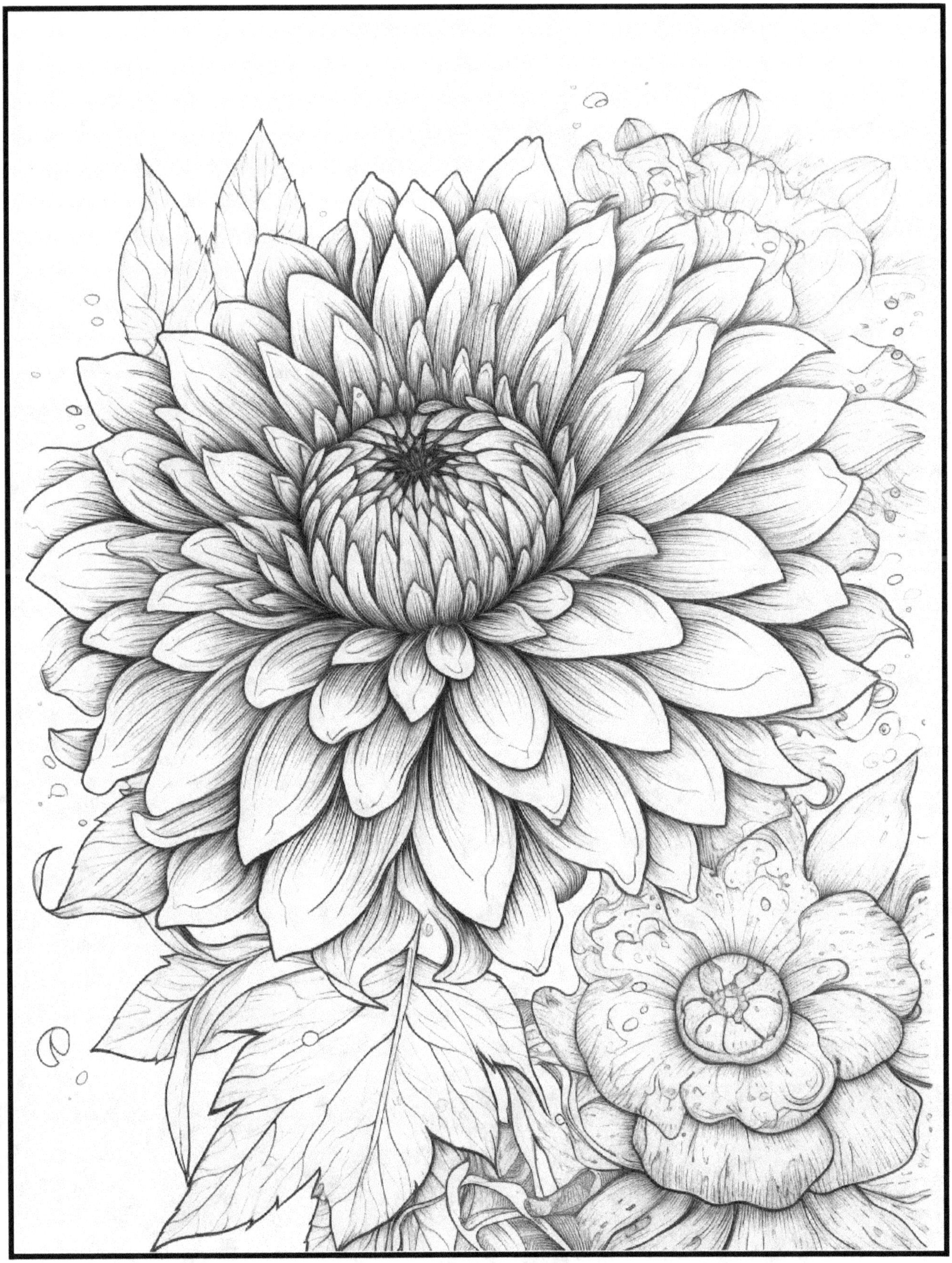

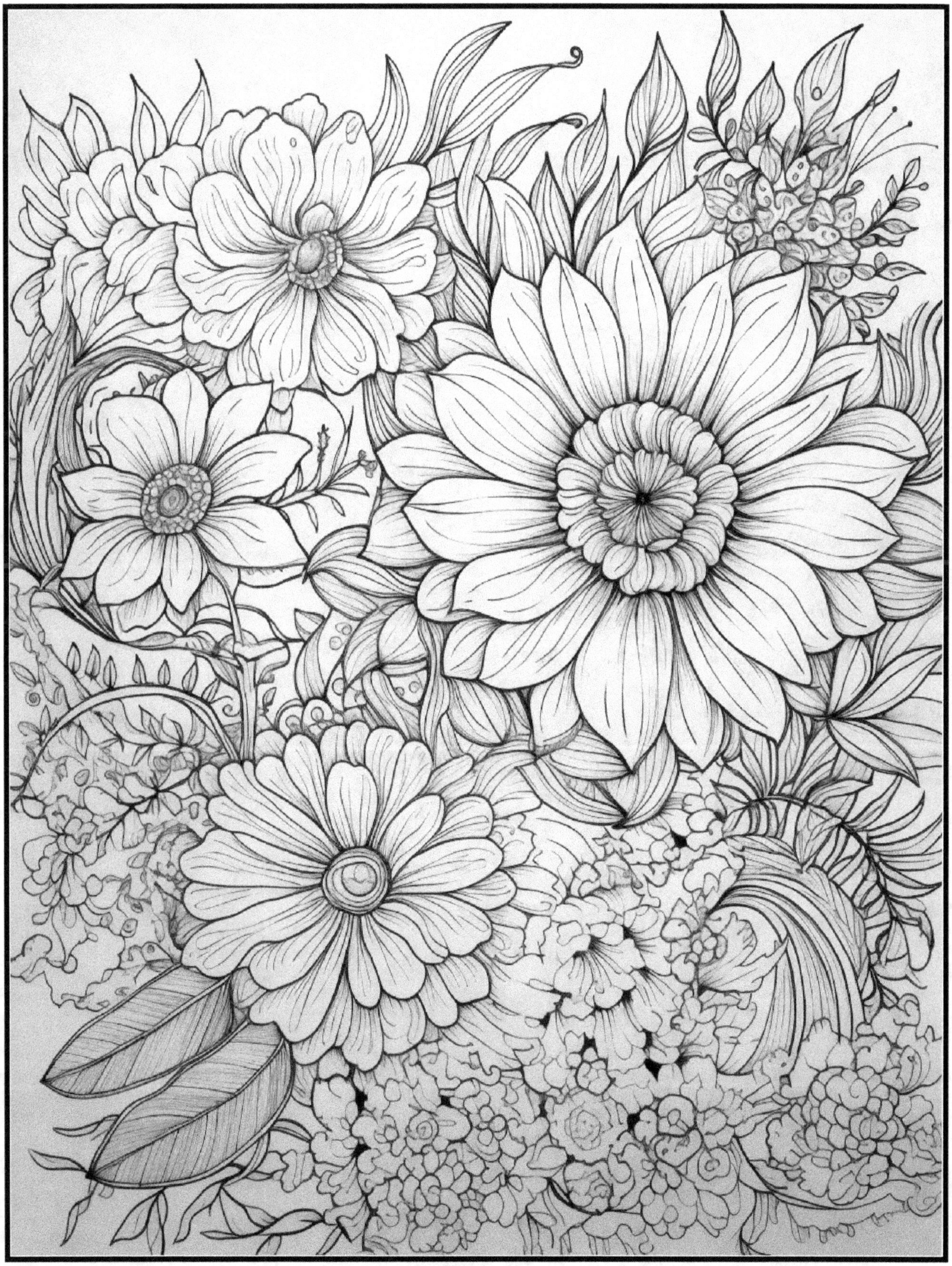

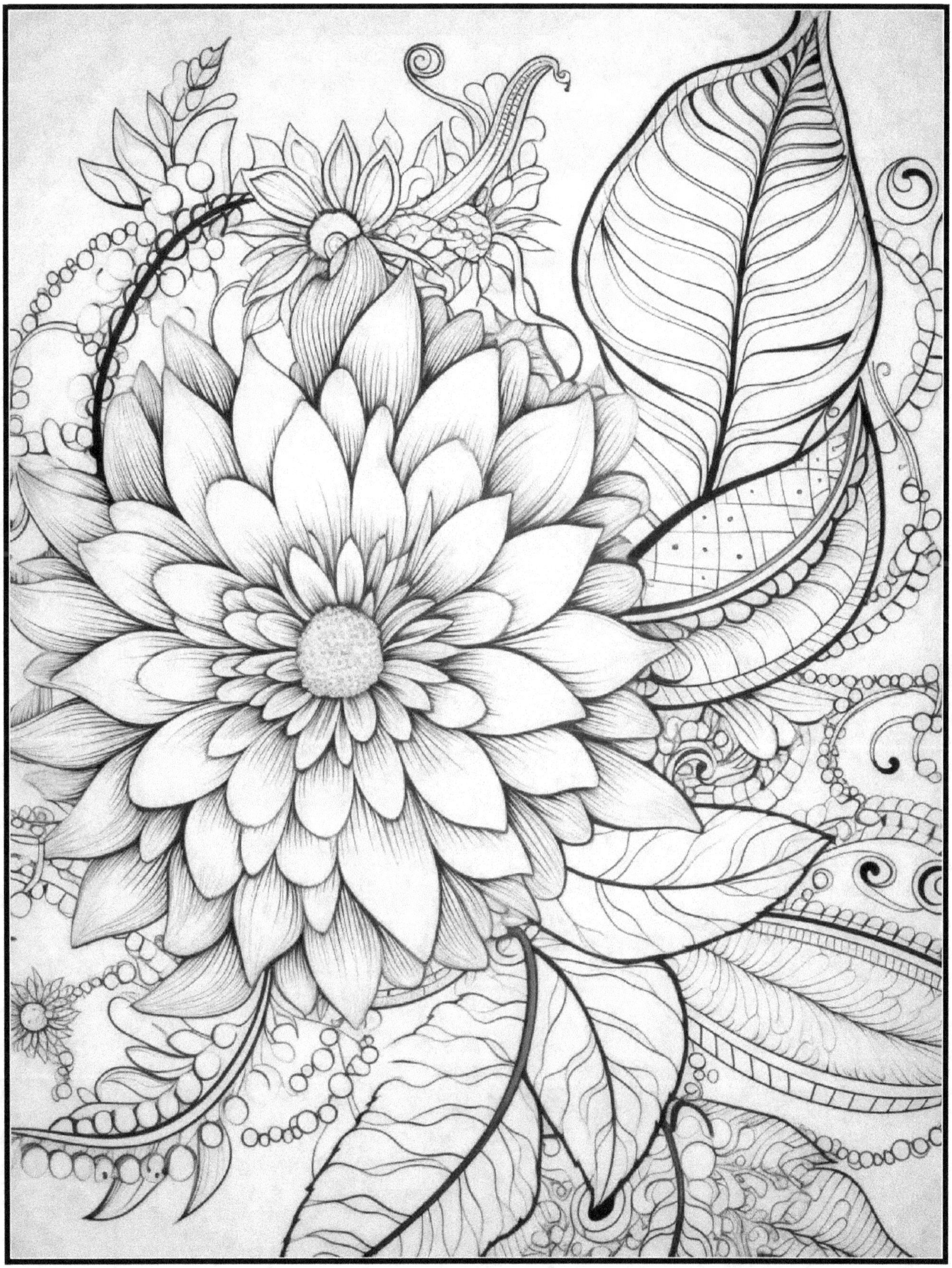

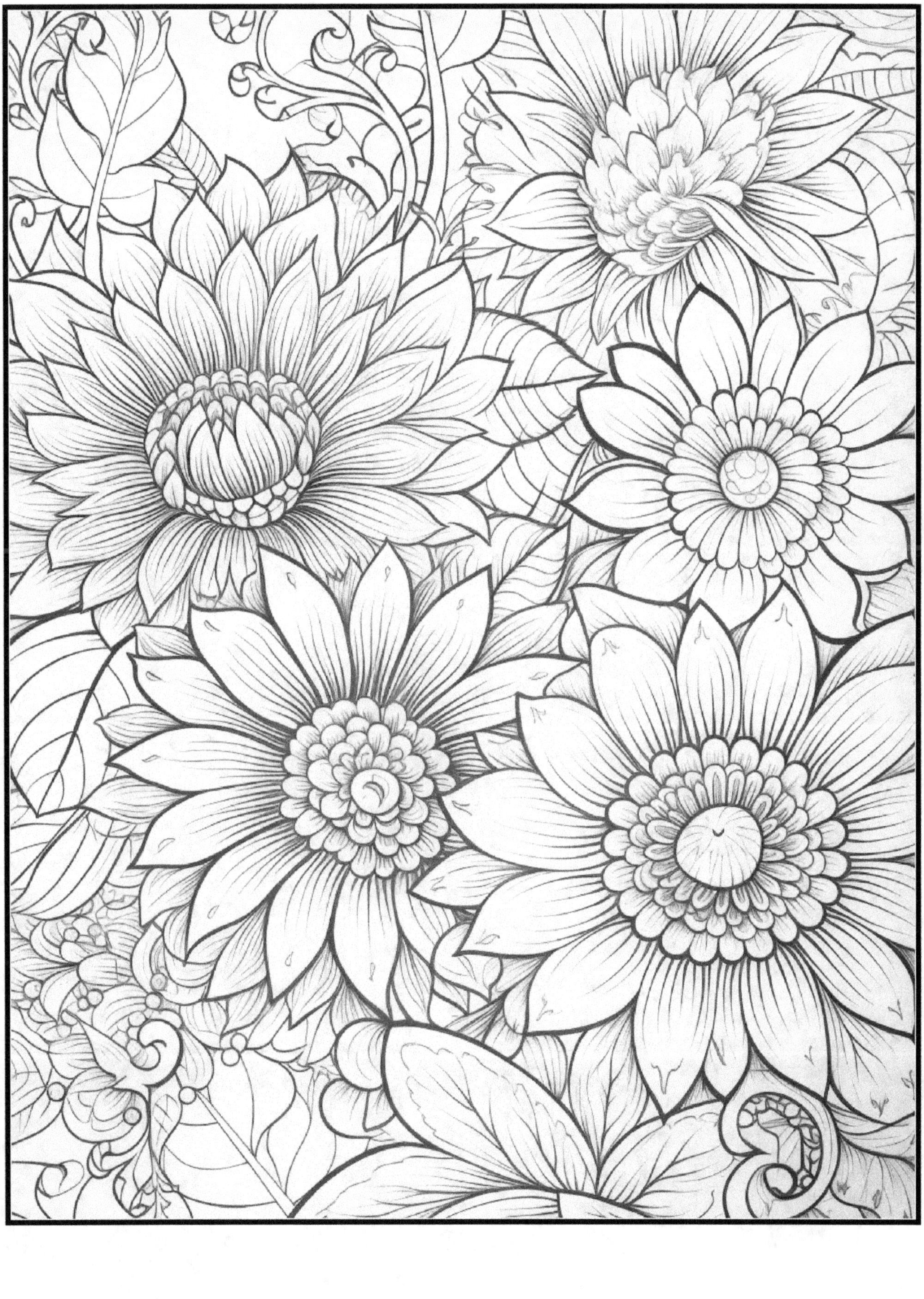

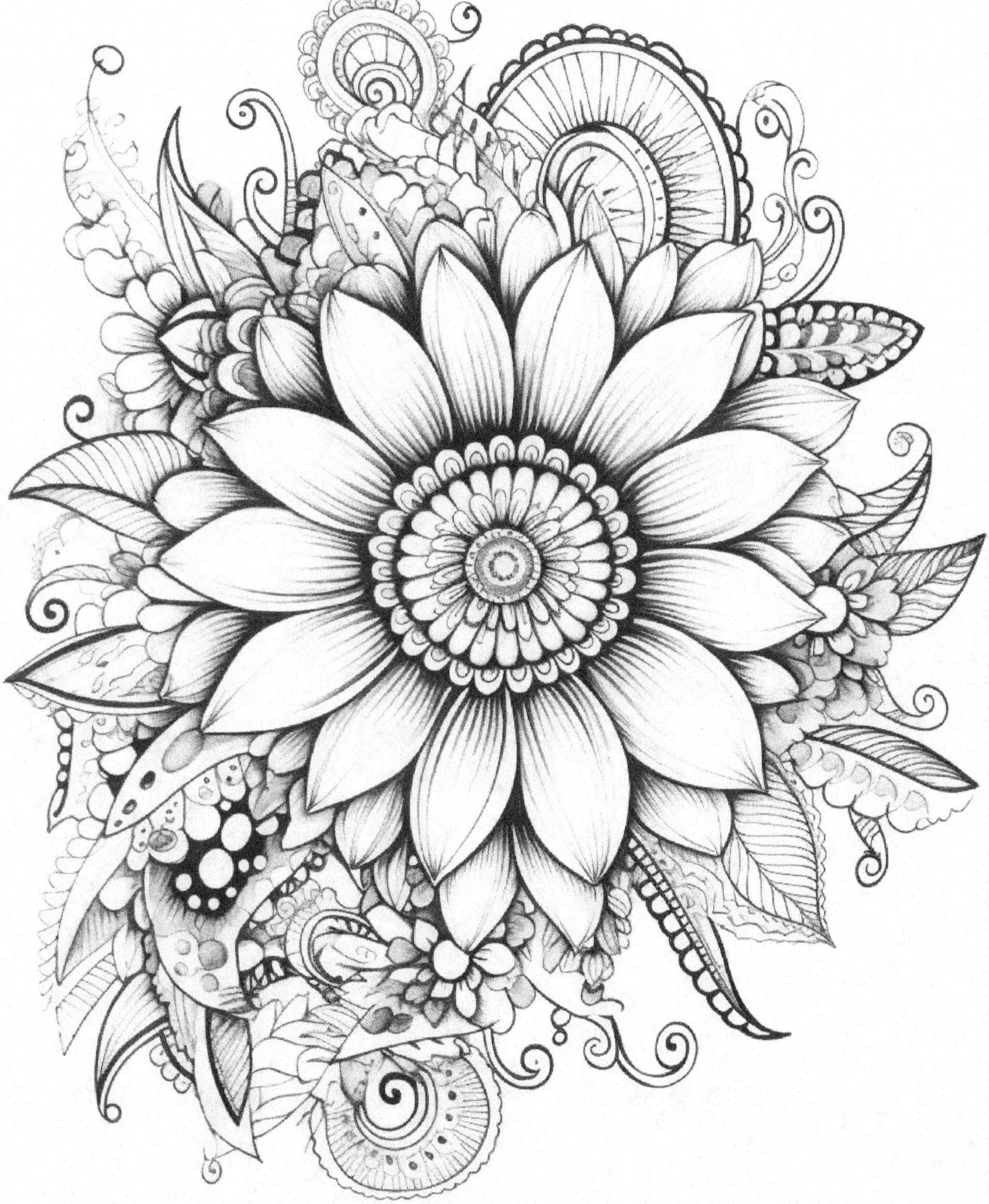

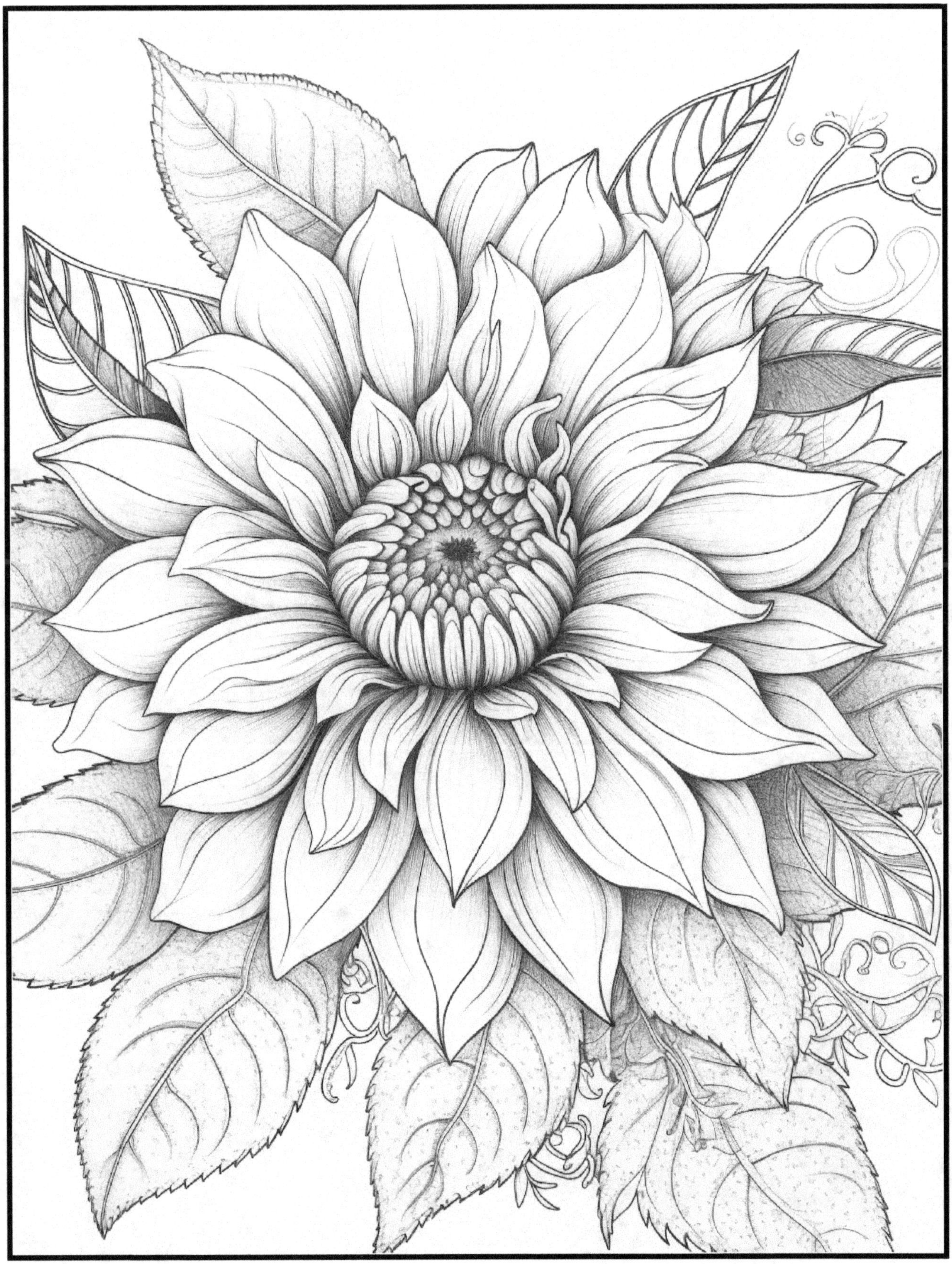

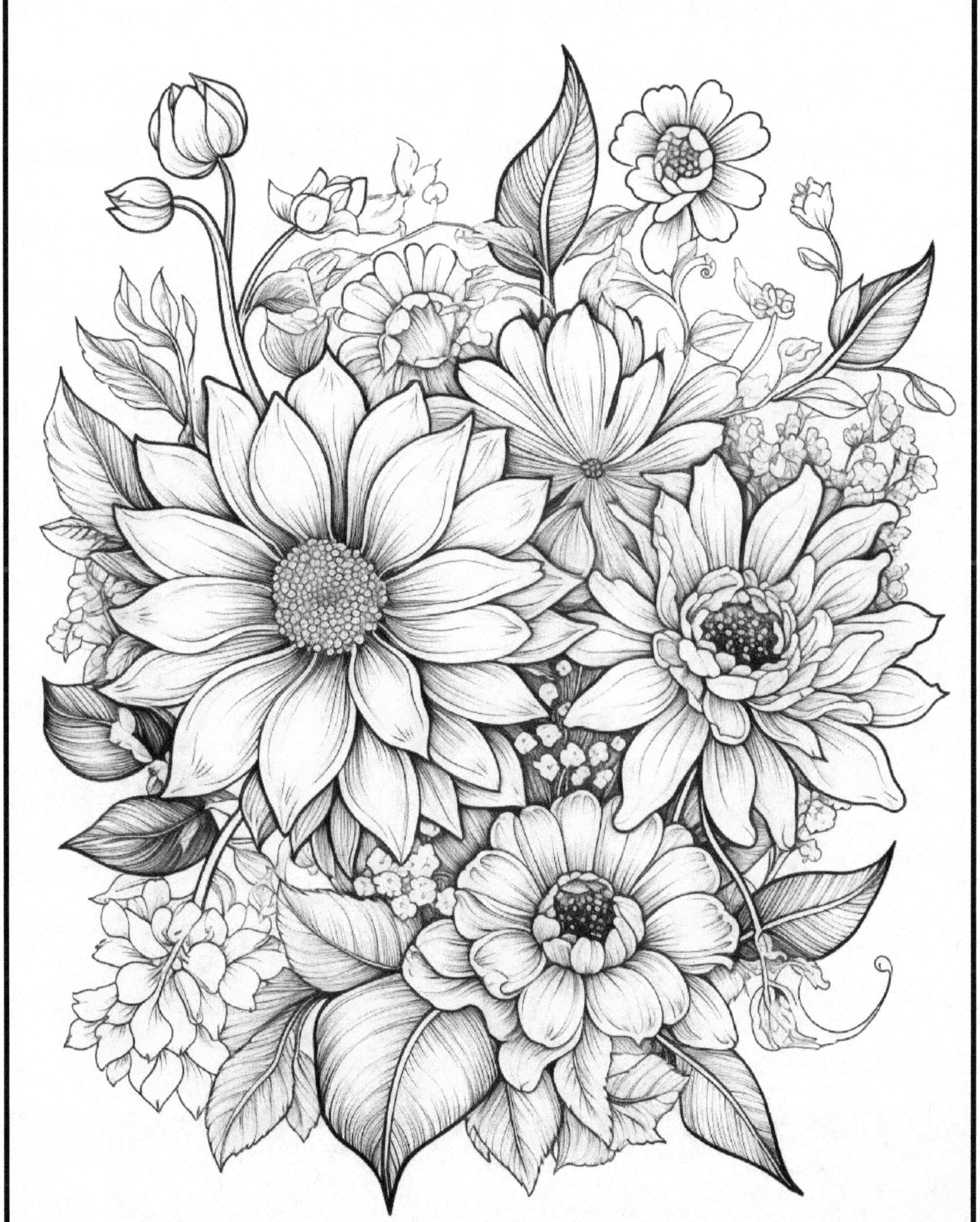

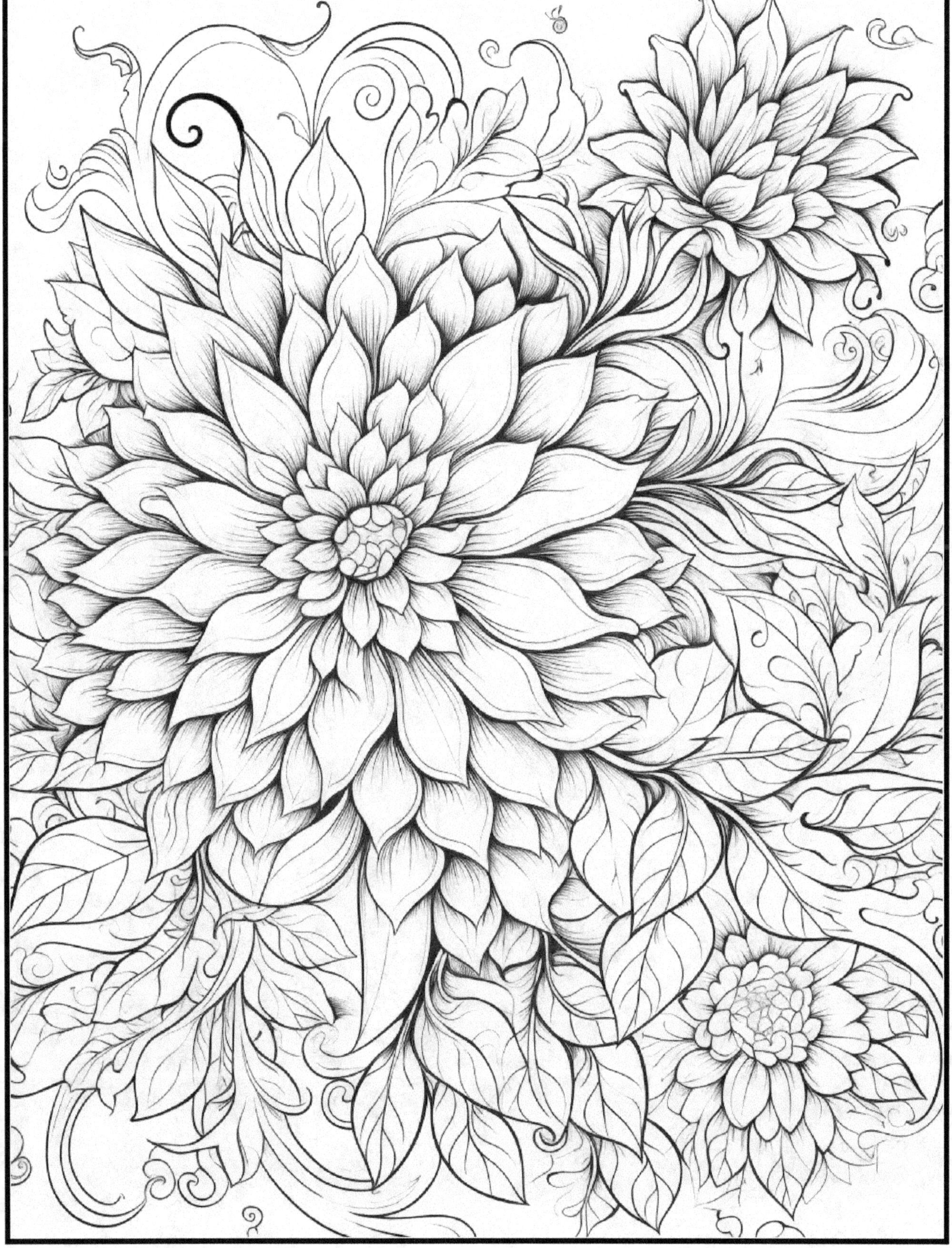

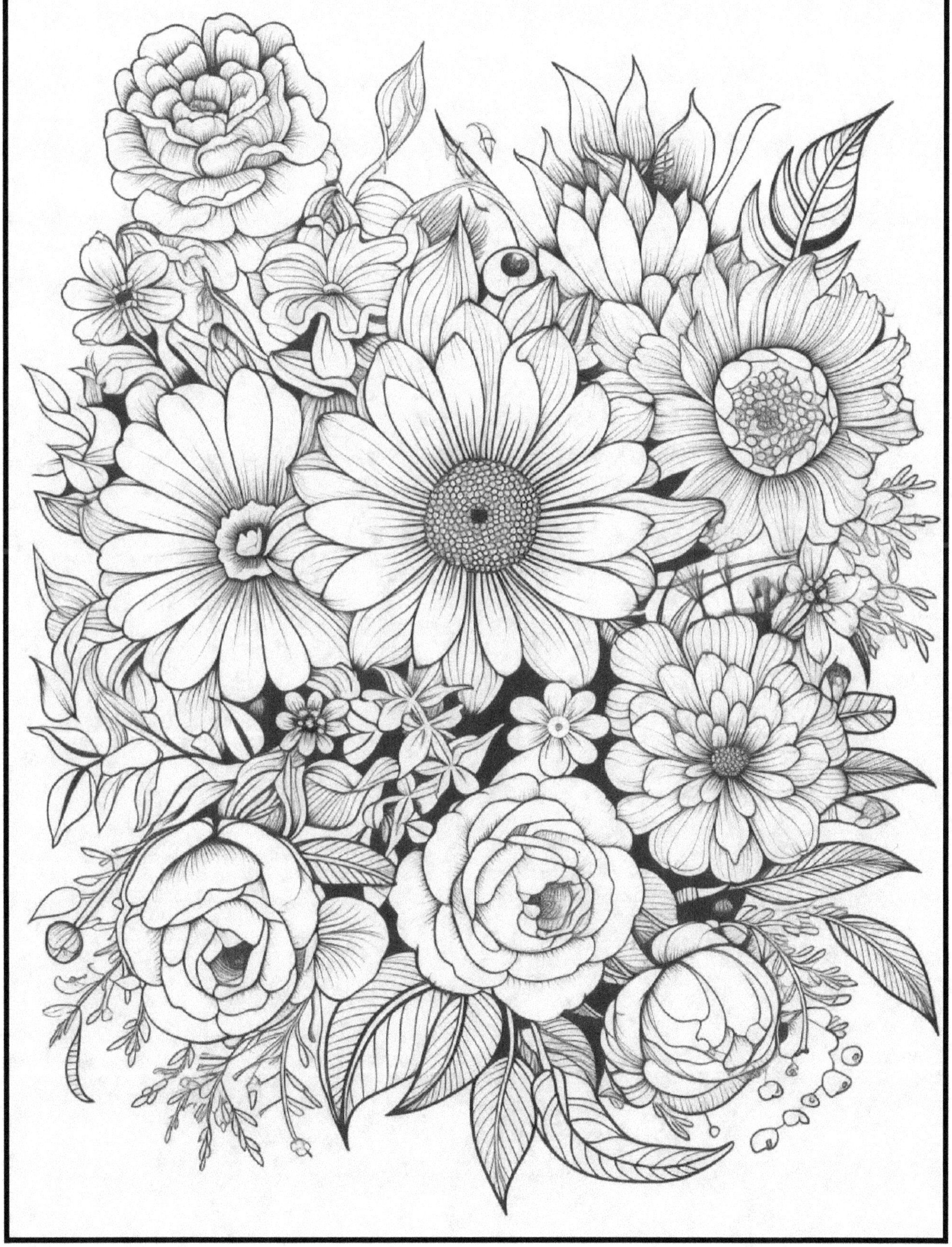

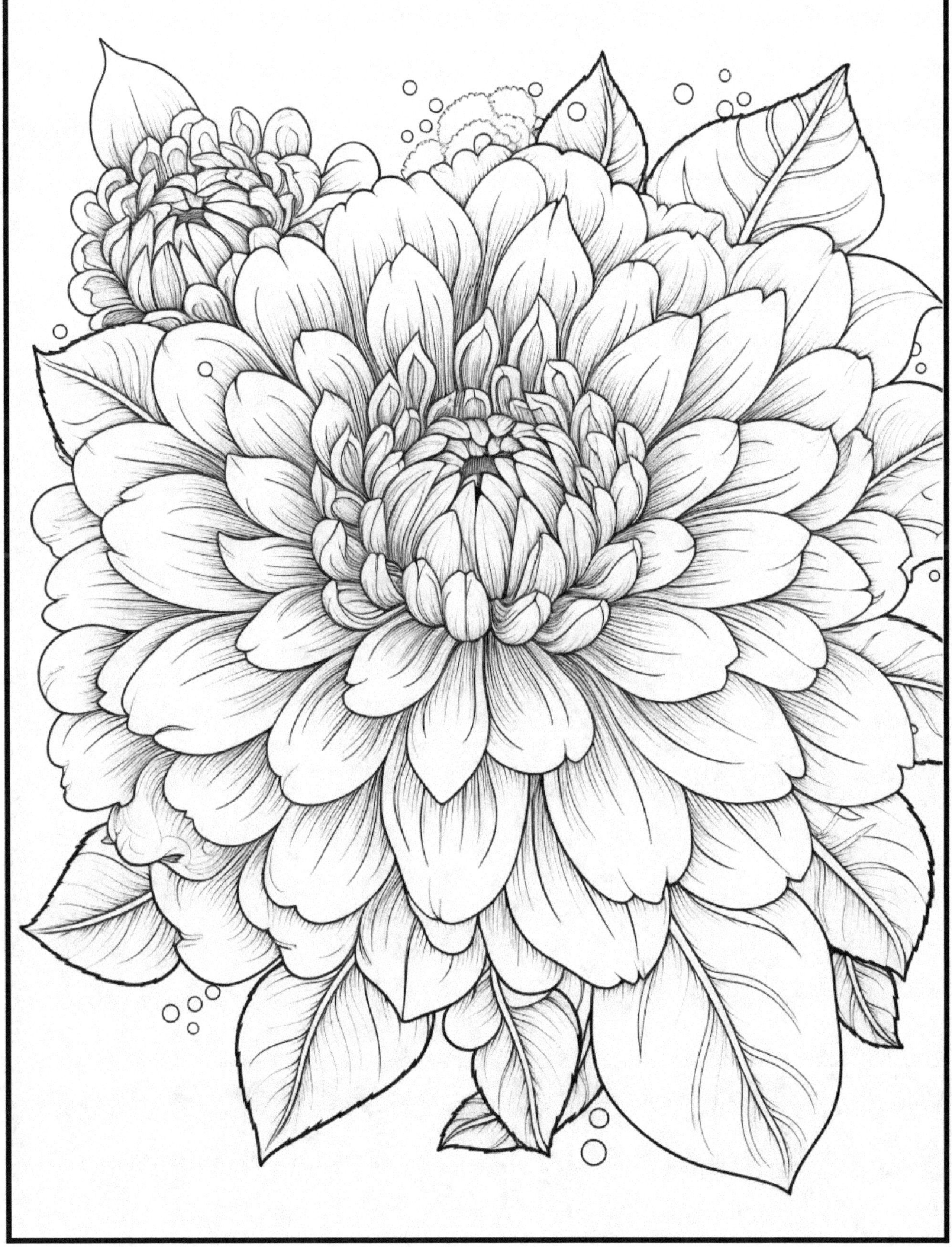

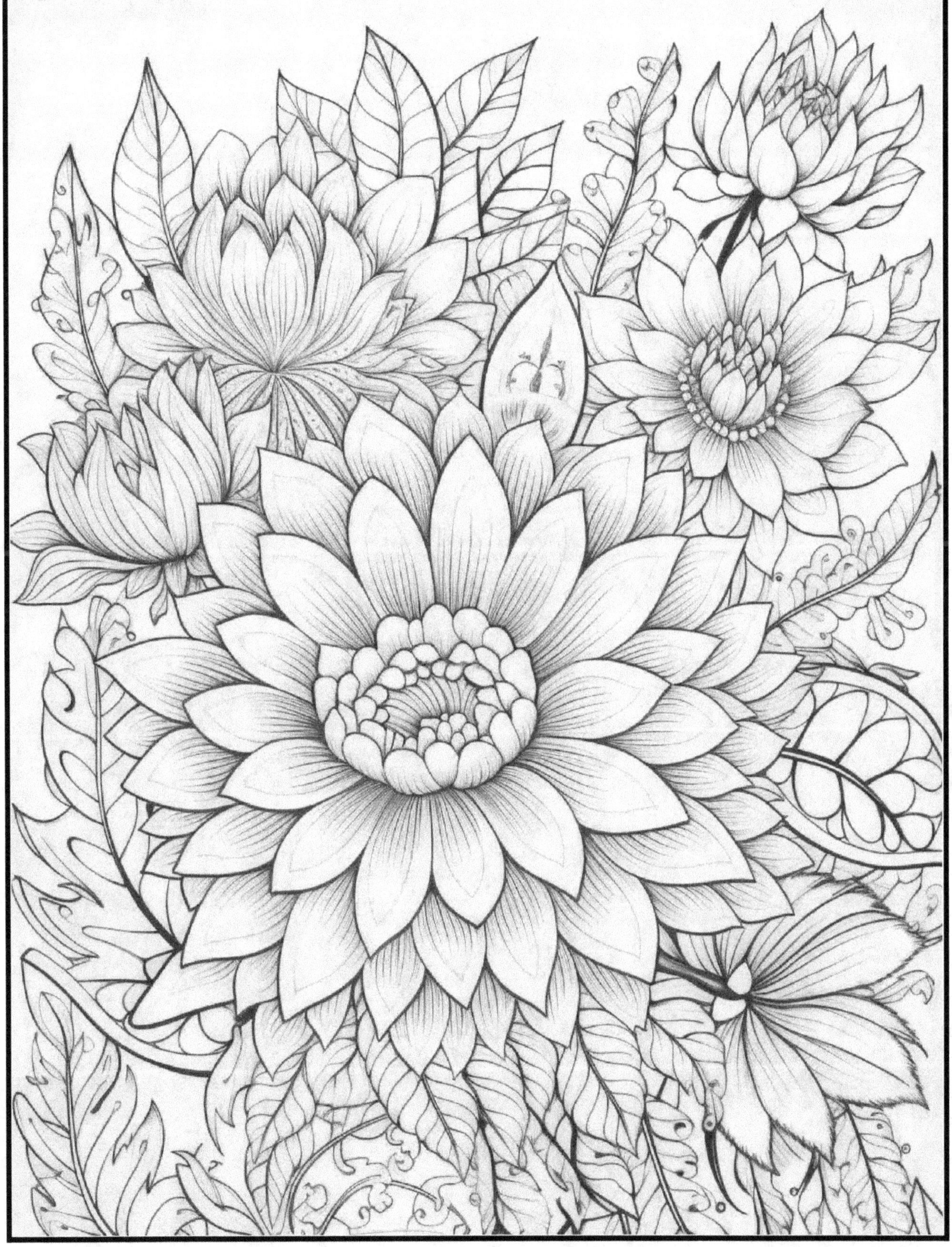

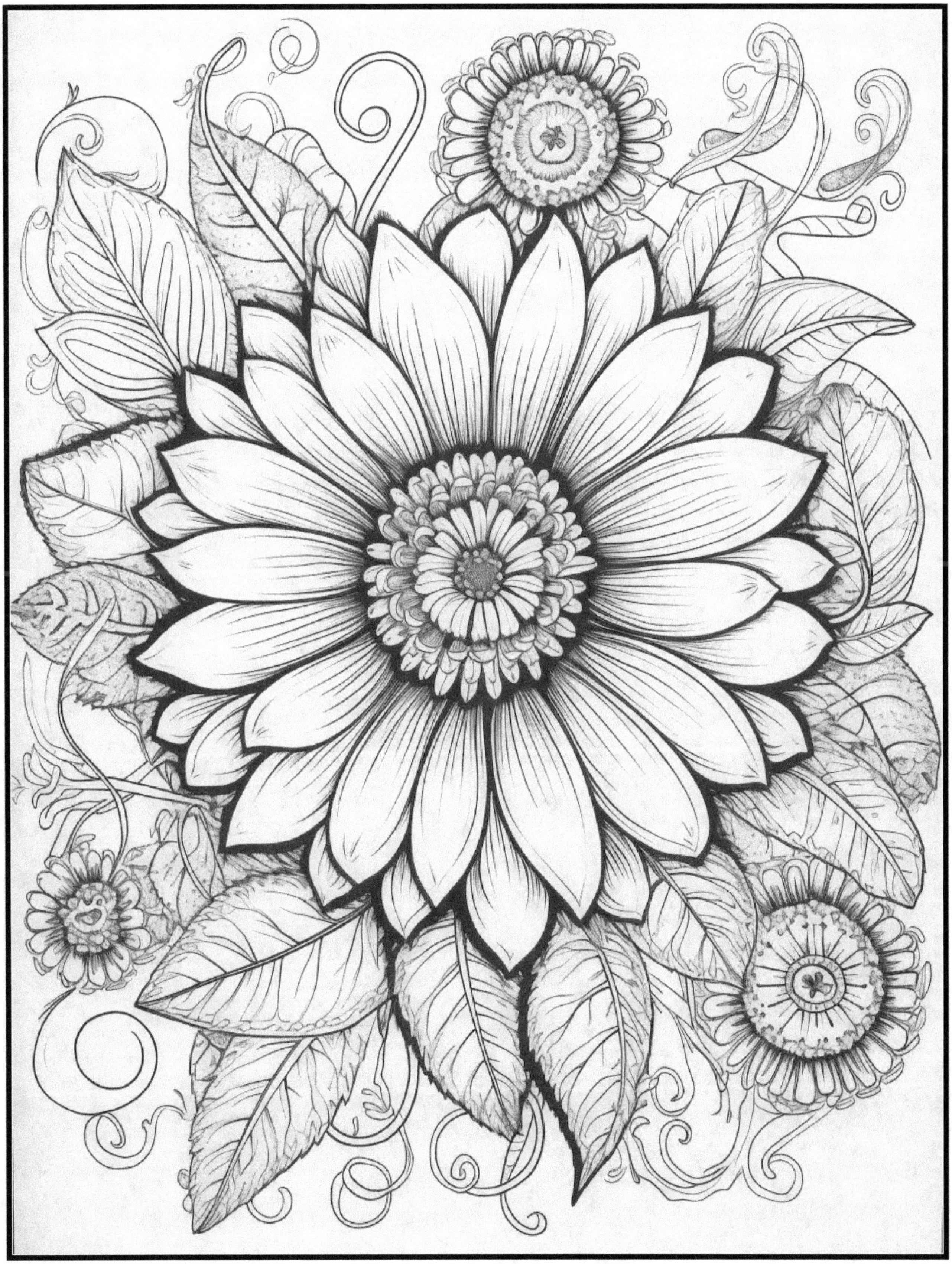

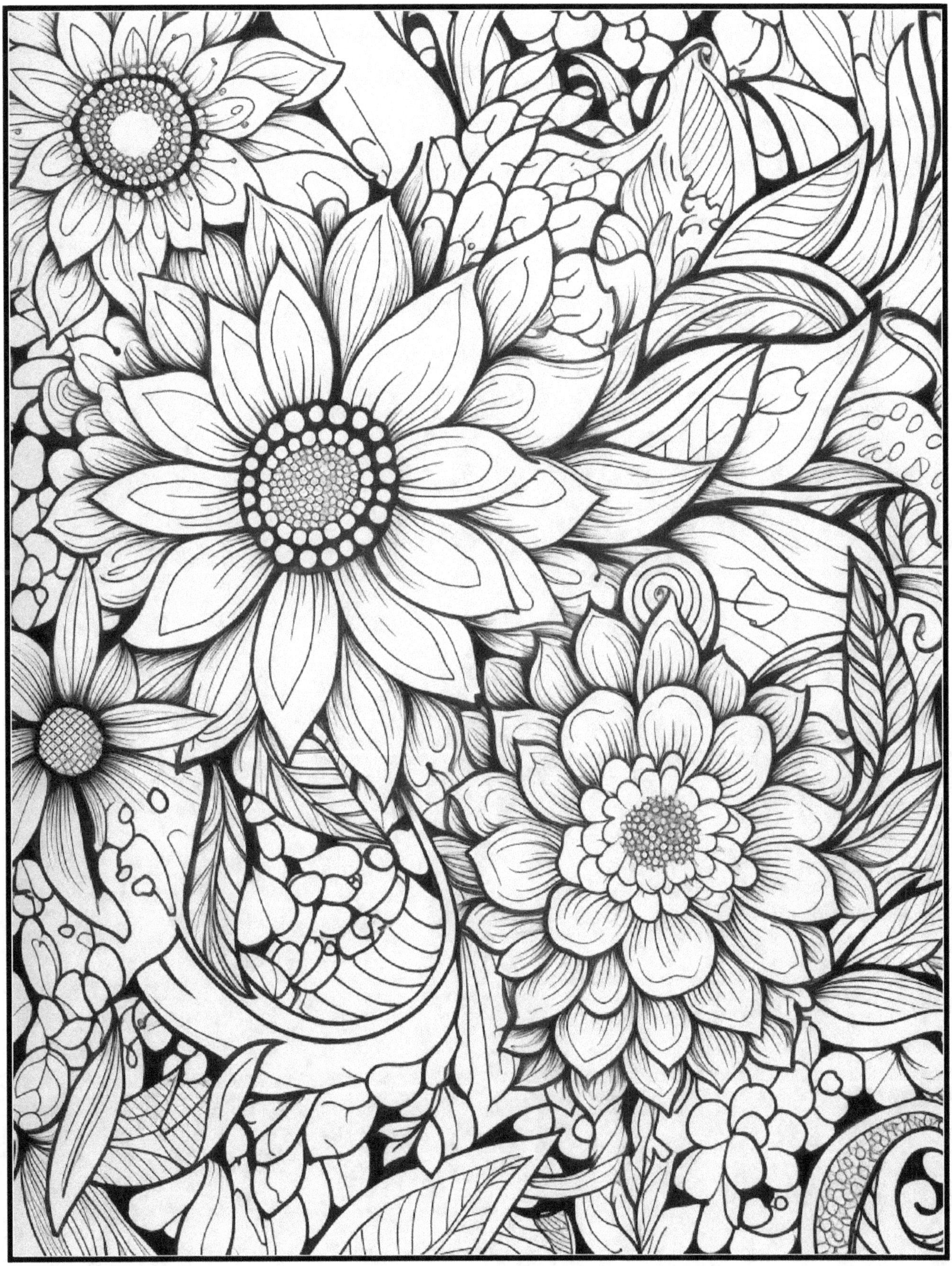

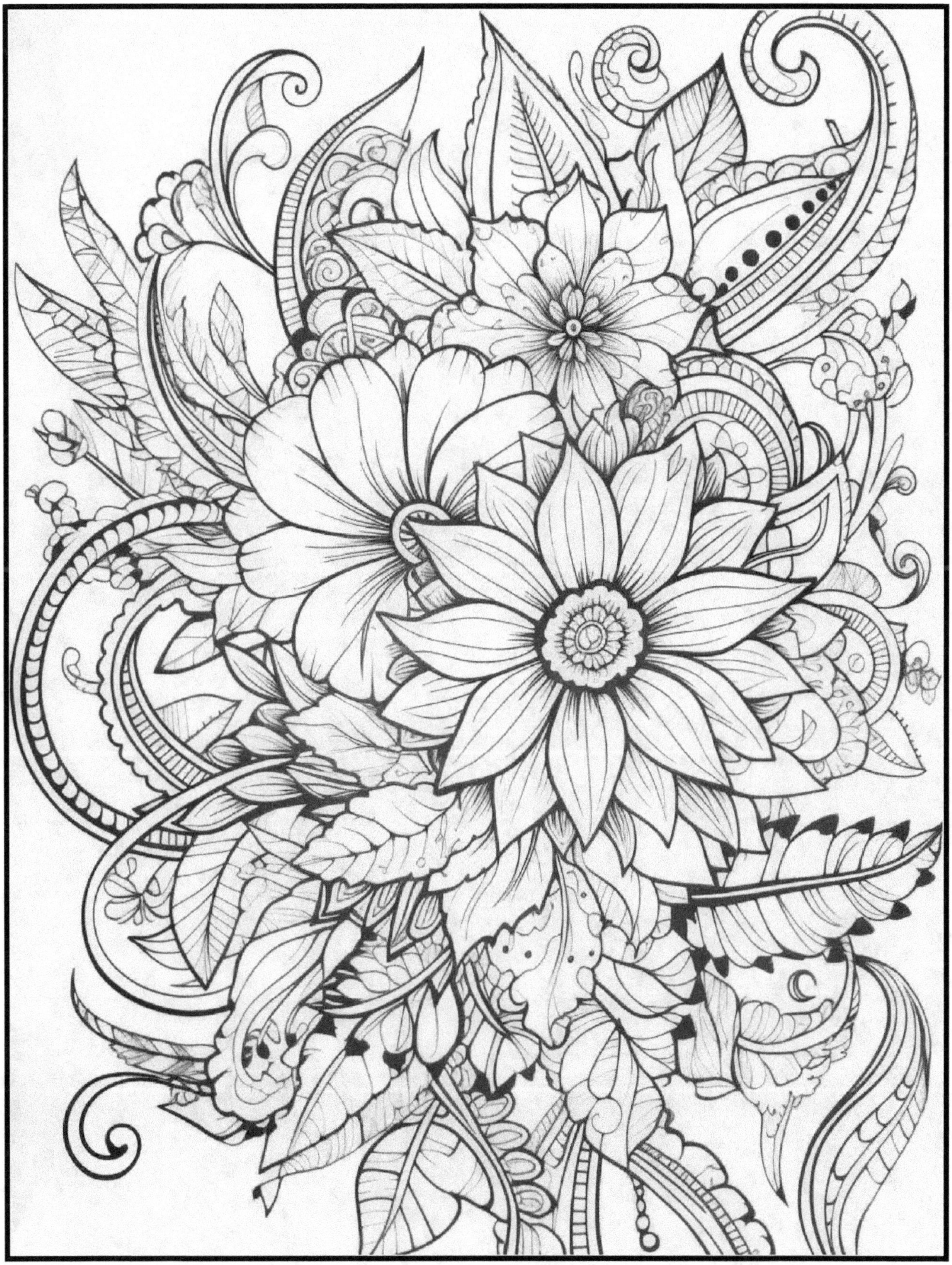

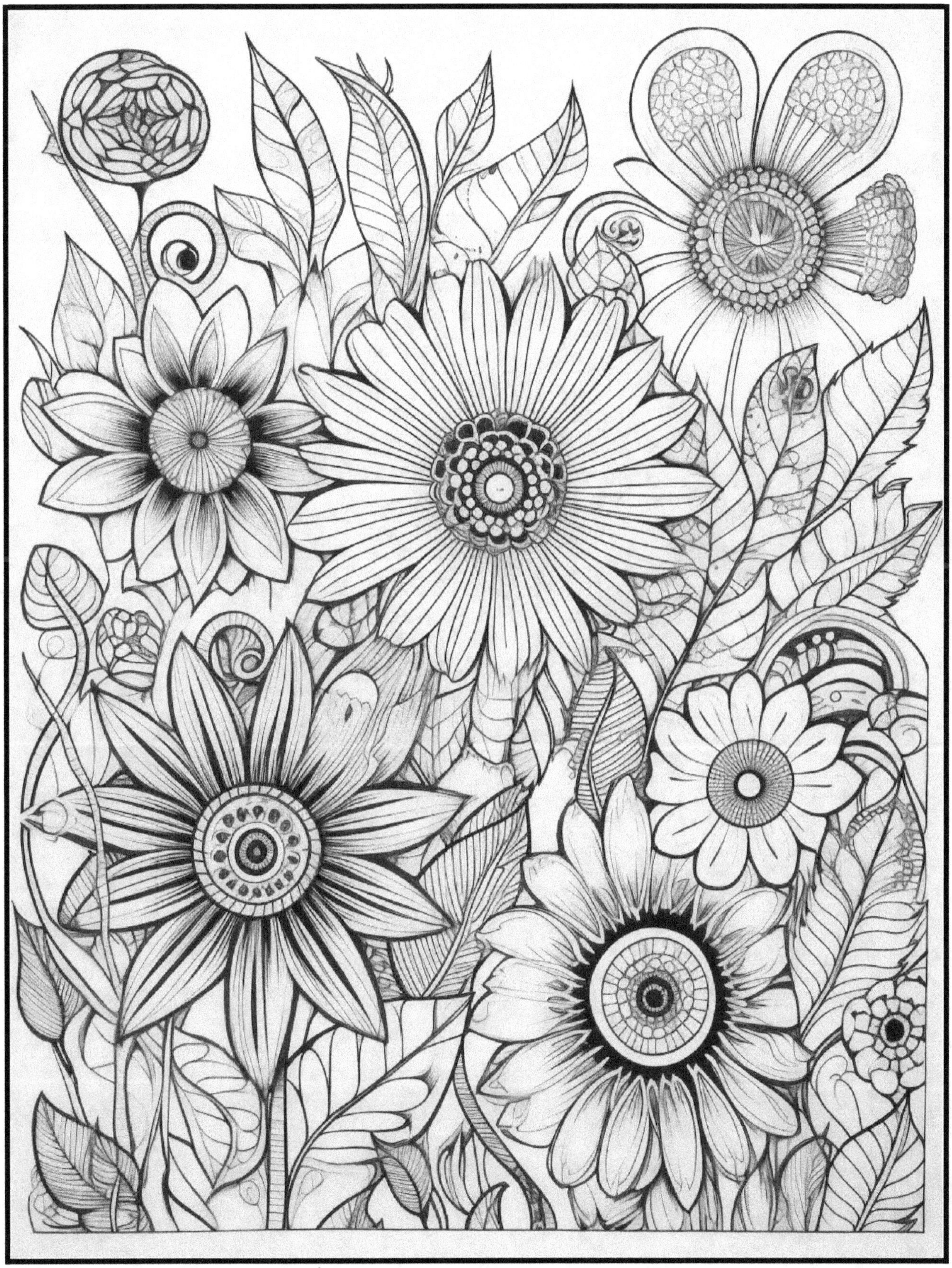

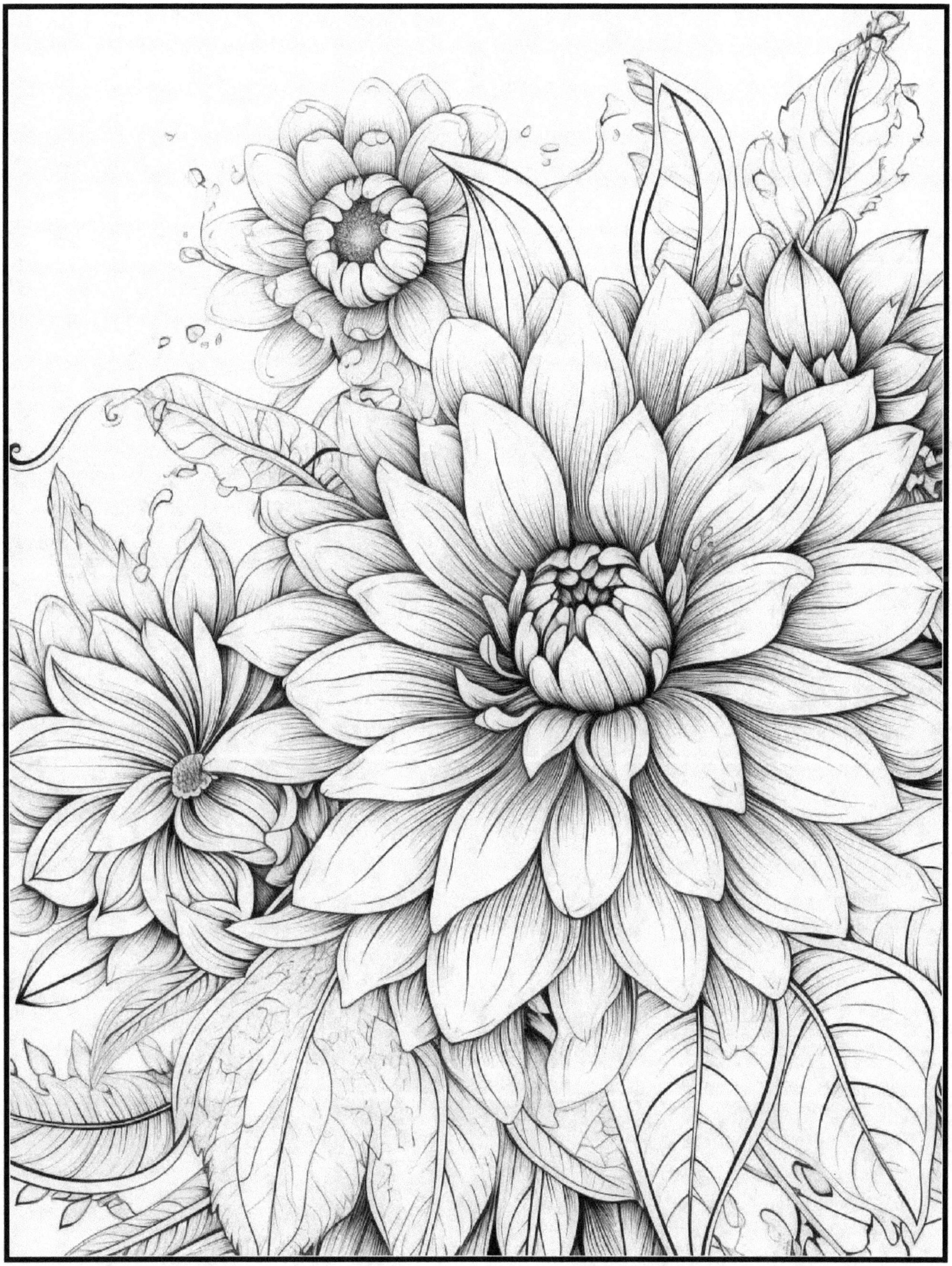

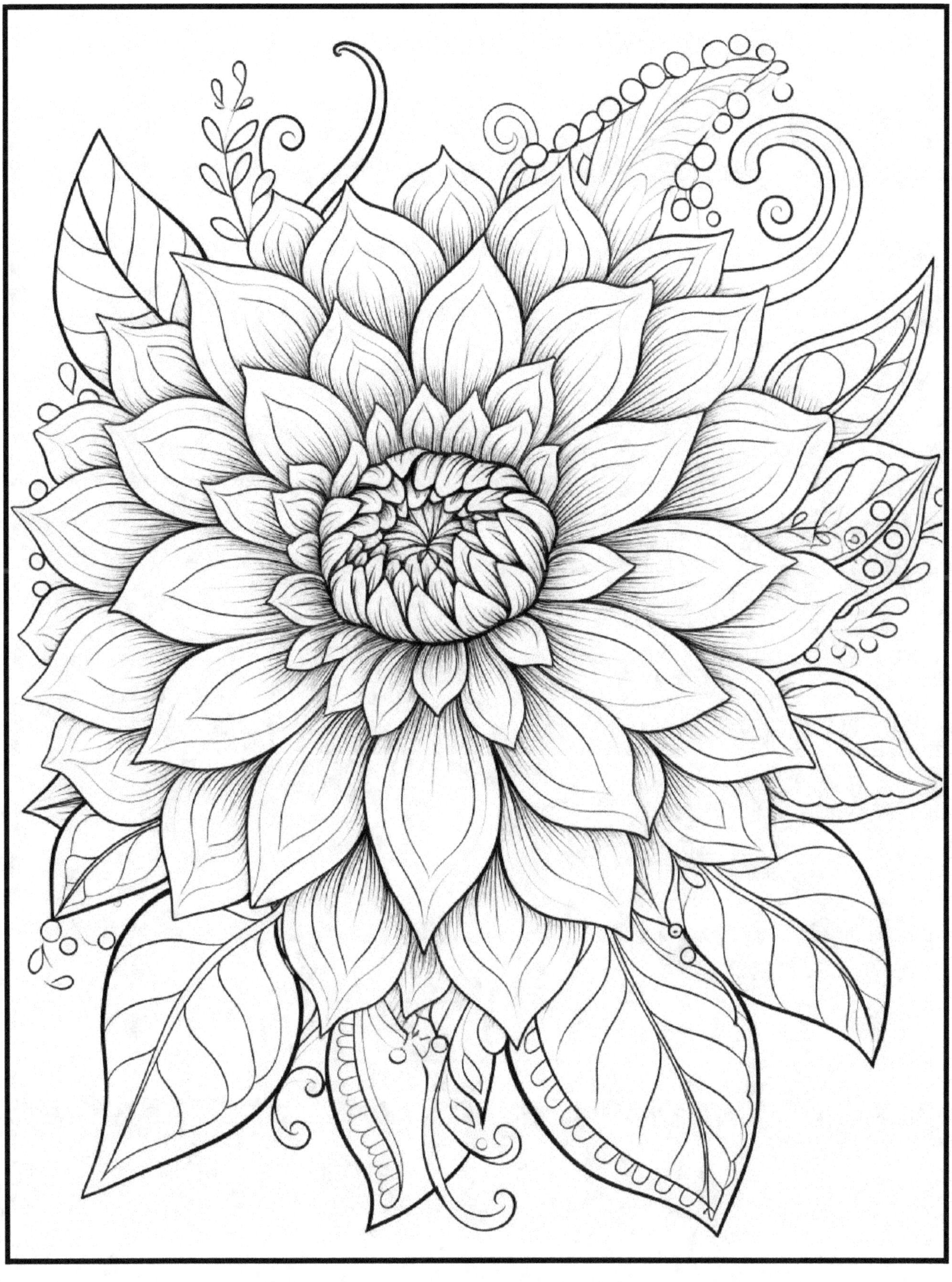

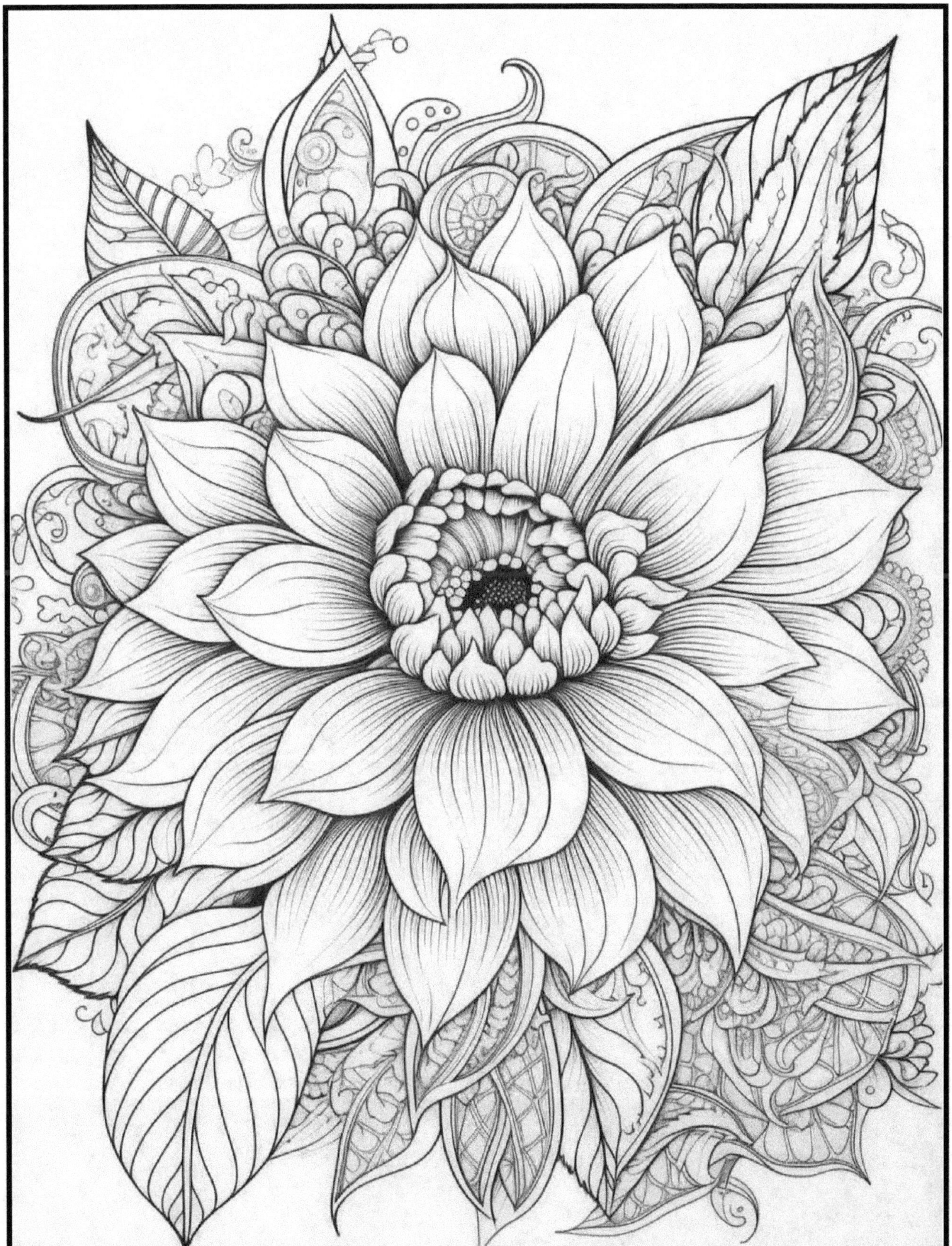

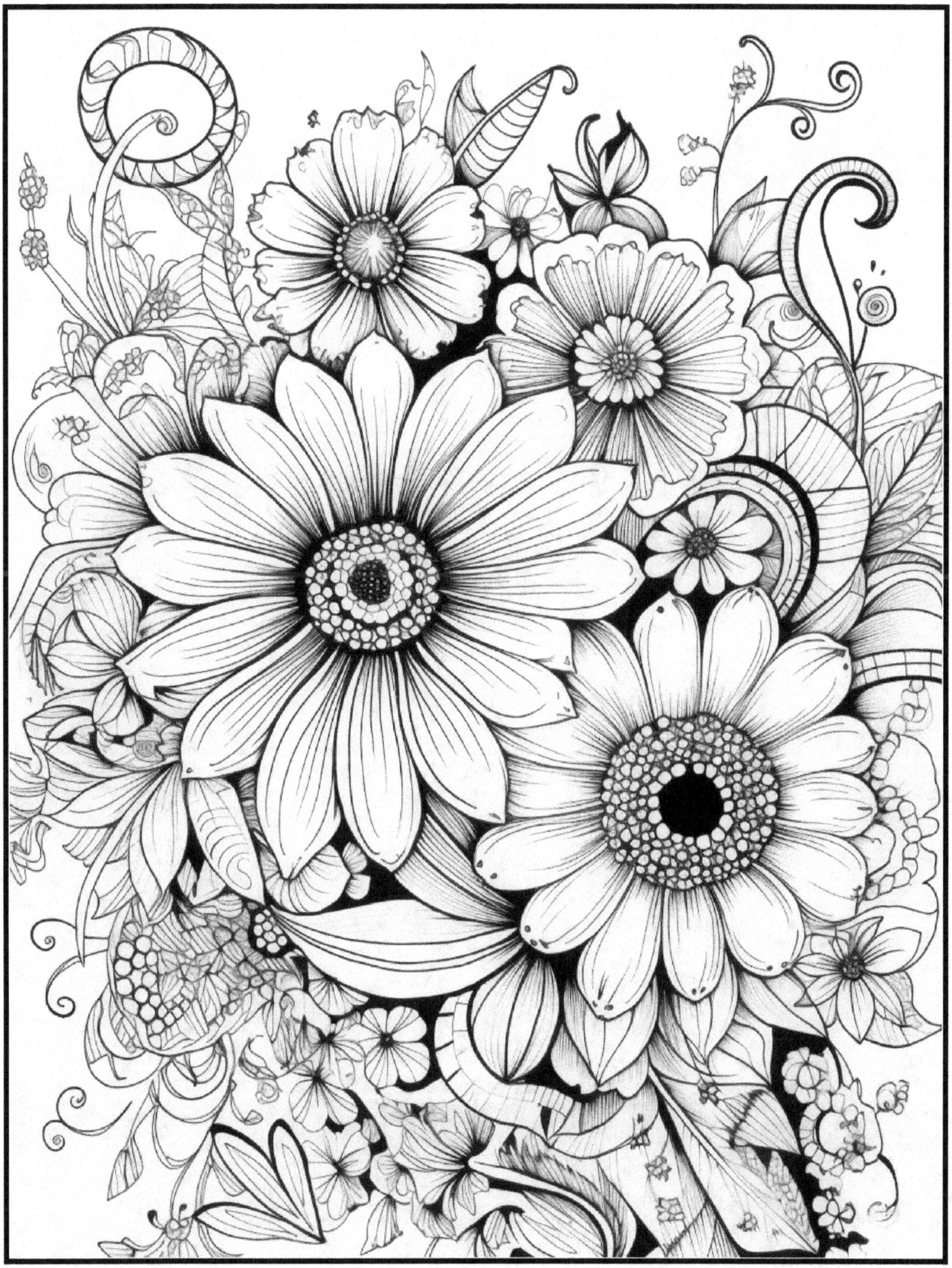

color test pages

color test pages

color test pages

color test pages

www.ingramcontent.com/pod-product-compliance
Lightning Source LLC
Chambersburg PA
CBHW080557220526
45466CB00010B/3180
* 9 7 9 8 3 9 3 6 7 8 5 0 0 *